MW01688024

STUDENT NAME: ______________________________

FIVE MINUTE DRILL

~~Daily~~ FUN! Classroom Routines for Percussion

Ralph Hicks
& Eric Rath

tapspace™ creativity in percussion™

FIVE MINUTE DRILL • TSPB-22

www.tapspace.com

Music, text, and photo content by Ralph Hicks and Eric Rath.

Cover design by Jesse Mattson (**www.jessemattson.com**).

Book layout, editing, and design by Murray Gusseck and Jim Casella.

Note: Errata and additions to this text, if any, may be found by visiting the "Errata" forum board on the Tapspace Forum at **www.tapspace.com/forums**

TABLE OF CONTENTS

ABOUT THE AUTHORS

First and foremost a teacher, **Ralph Hicks** feels blessed to have been influenced by amazing and dedicated educators. Ralph is a product of the highly successful Spring High School Band program (Spring, Texas), winning two Texas 5A State Marching Championships, one BOA Grand National Championship, a PAS Call for Tapes, and a naming to the 1995 Texas All-State Orchestra.

Receiving a full scholarship to the University of Kentucky, Ralph studied percussion under Professor James B. Campbell. In 1996, he took first place in the PAS International Vibraphone Solo competition. In 1997, he was a member of the Cavaliers Drum & Bugle Corps and was named a Yamaha Young Performing Artist.

Ralph teaches at Mitchell Intermediate in The Woodlands, Texas. He is director of The Percussion Studio community performance group and founder of "Let Them Drum!"—a non-profit organization providing drum therapy services for children and adults with special needs, memory care and assisted living, and addiction recovery. In 2012, Mr. Hicks was named Mitchell Intermediate's Teacher of the Year and Conroe ISD Outstanding Teacher in the Arts by The Woodlands Waterway Arts Council.

Ralph lives in his hometown of Spring, Texas, with his wife Marcail and their two children, Brooklynn and William. He is a member of Phi Mu Alpha Sinfonia, Texas Music Educators Association, the Percussive Arts Society, the Drum Circle Facilitators Guild, the American Society of Composers, Authors and Publishers, and is endorsed by Innovative Percussion.

Eric Rath is an active educator, clinician, arranger, and composer. In addition to his day-to-day duties as a music educator, Mr. Rath serves as Adjunct Instructor of Percussion at Amarillo College.

Mr. Rath is a graduate of West Texas A&M University, where he received both his Bachelor of Music Education and his Master of Arts degree. While at WT, he studied percussion with Dr. Susan Martin Tariq and was a member of the symphonic band under the direction of Dr. Gary Garner, then Mr. Don Lefevre.

As a composer, Mr. Rath has a growing list of original works and arrangements published through TRN Music, C. Alan Publications, Tapspace Publications, HoneyRock Publications, and Eric Rath Music. Mr. Rath's compositions have been performed at the Midwest Clinic and the Texas Music Educators Association Convention. Mr. Rath, along with Ralph Hicks, is co-author of the percussion ensemble collection ***Beyond Basic Percussion: Developing Independence Through Ensemble Performance*** (Tapspace Publications).

Mr. Rath is a member of the Amarillo Symphony Orchestra and also regularly performs with the Amarillo Opera. Mr. Rath is active as an in-demand freelance percussionist as well as a member on the worship team at his church. He is also a former member of the Phantom Regiment Drum & Bugle Corps.

Mr. Rath resides in Amarillo, Texas, with his wife Kayla and their children Regan, Grant, and McKinley. His professional affiliations include the Percussive Arts Society, Texas Music Educators Association, Texas Bandmasters Association. He is an alumnus and former chapter president of Phi Mu Alpha Sinfonia. He is also proud to be an Innovative Percussion Artist as well as a member of the American Society of Composers, Authors and Publishers (ASCAP).

INTRODUCTION

The ***FIVE MINUTE DRILL*** concept was put together for a clinic at the 2012 Texas Music Educators Association's (TMEA) annual convention entitled *Beyond the Back of the Room: After the Beginning Percussion Year*. Through years of observing successful Texas band directors, such as Bill Watson, Andy Sealy, and Joni Perez, the one constant we found was a rigorous "daily drill" routine. On average, 25 percent of each rehearsal was being dedicated solely to the fundamentals—long tones, lip slurs, articulation studies, etc. While part of our TMEA clinic was based on our book *Beyond Basic Percussion,* the concept of a daily "five minute drill" was something our own students were quickly benefitting from.

While lip slurs and long tones help develop invaluable skills on wind instruments, they do little for the needs of the percussion section. Many successful programs find ways to involve percussionists, but often this entails merely doubling the flute part on a keyboard or tasking a player to play simple rhythms on a snare drum or practice pad. The percussionists in the class soon realize that all the other musicians are working essential skills on their instruments while they are only being kept busy. No wonder they start messing around!

Knowing that this is a common problem, we thought we could use part of our clinic to help offer some solutions. We used Mitchell Intermediate (The Woodlands, Texas), which had 35-minute classes, for our model. After factoring in time for setup and teardown of both class equipment AND pulling out instruments, **we built five solid minutes to focus solely on essential percussion techniques not typically covered in the normal daily drill routine for the winds.** In order to maximize our time, we streamlined our exercises to those techniques most commonly used. We wanted a solid foundation of terminology, sticking options, muscle development, and rudimental vocabulary that would turn even the most casual players into valuable contributors.

FIVE MINUTE DRILL engages young percussionists in a way not possible in a full band setting. Rather than feeling like you're just "keeping them busy," you'll know that you're providing attention equal to that of your wind players in the development of their basic skills.

Using *FMD* as a curriculum for basic percussion fundamentals throughout the district, high schools and their feeders can vertically align their essential techniques and terminology. When a middle school student starts high school, they'll already know what to expect! The exercises in this book also provide an exciting new resource for private lesson settings.

We feel strongly that players learn more when what they're working on is fun! *FMD* makes it fun for students and teachers, and it can be fun for audiences, too. Need a class feature for a concert, faculty meeting, or band party? Look no further!

A strong regimen of daily fundamentals can significantly improve percussionists' concept of sound and technique in a relatively short period of time. Whether it be before, during, or after school, in private lessons, or at home, the skills developed with *FMD* will take percussionists far ***beyond the back of the room!***

HOW TO USE THIS BOOK

At its core, ***FIVE MINUTE DRILL*** is a series of individual exercises and sequences for both practice pad and mallet keyboard accompanied by play-along audio tracks. It is designed to be ***fun*** for percussion students while encouraging a consistent practice routine. It can be used both in and out of the classroom.

In the classroom, *FMD* can provide percussion students with something productive to do during class time, separate from the wind players who are going through their own fundamental drills. The students will have the option of practicing rudiments on the practice pad or major/chromatic scales on the keyboard. The play-along tracks are designed to enable the students to do one or two drills each as time allows.

In the private teaching setting, *FMD* can be used with students one-on-one to augment their teacher's own program...helping to knock out some of the fundamentals in a way that is fun but not overly "mental."

To help maximize what you can do with ***FIVE MINUTE DRILL,*** here are some general guidelines on how it was meant to be used:

Have a plan

The ultimate goal should be a regular rotation of the full *Five Minute Drill* sequences. As your students progress toward being able to play the full sequences using the slower "breakdown" exercises, figure out how much time you have and combine the exercises to fit your needs. The key to success will be both **variety**— mixing up the instruments and exercises day-by-day—and **consistency**— keeping a normal routine.

Here's an example of a varied routine to keep things consistent and fun over the course of a week.

Monday	Tuesday	Wednesday	Thursday	Friday
Stay with Band* double flute part on keyboard (to work on roll techniques)	**Five Minute Drill PRACTICE PAD** • Legato Strokes & Dynamics - med • Flams & Paradiddles - slow	**Five Minute Drill KEYBOARDS** • F Major, Bb Major - slow • Chromatic C Full Sequence - med	**Five Minute Drill PRACTICE PAD** • Timing Patterns - slow • Double Strokes - med	**Stay with Band*** accessory routine

**see opposite page*

In addition to school or private lessons, *FMD* is also an ideal model for an at-home practice regimen. Just because students are told how long to practice each day or week doesn't necessarily mean they know what to do for that length of time. For younger students, 20 minutes of "practice time" can turn into five minutes of actual work followed by 15 minutes of goofing off. The **Data Tracking Tools** *(described on page 45)* on the CD-ROM provide an easy way to track practice time at home or in the classroom. Kids are really busy these days, and a little help in structure and efficiency will be appreciated by both students and parents.

Take your time and track your data

There is a lot of material to cover within *FMD*, especially if these techniques are new to players. There are plenty of track combinations to get your allotted time in, so mix it up and try not to rush the process. Start with the slower *Breakdown* tracks and the included Data Tracking Tools to record your progress. It will take some getting used to, but after a few weeks you will start to see some patterns emerge. Tracking data allows you to analyze your progress and make any necessary adjustments.

Follow the stickings

While it may seem inconvenient for a young player to follow stickings at first, the indicated stickings have been designed with specific goals in mind. They are crucial in developing muscle memory. Don't cut corners here. If a sticking is inconvenient, it's probably identifying something specific that you'll benefit from. We're experienced percussionists ourselves, and we can assure you that the included stickings will help develop techniques. Stick with it—you can thank us later!

Use the recordings

The tracks on the CD-ROM really do make a difference! Careful consideration went into matching the music with the concepts being addressed. The accompaniment also helps develop a sense of timing and ensemble awareness in a way a standard metronome cannot. Be cautious with the volume—don't crank the speakers so loud you can't hear the practice pads or keyboards. The slow tracks should be slow enough to use right out of the gate and could offer an opportunity to practice counting or verbal note naming as well.

*Staying with the Band

On days when the *FMD* routines aren't being used, band directors need to have productive things that percussionists do while the wind players practice their fundamentals. This is probably a topic for another book, but for starters, here are a few ideas to keep percussionists engaged:

- **Percussionists double the flute part** on keyboards (e.g., using smooth, connected rolls).
- **Devise an accessory routine** where percussionists rotate playing simple time-keeping parts on common accessory instruments like bass drum, snare drum, cymbals, triangle, and tambourine.

Are you a "lone wolf" band director?

If you don't have an assistant band director or percussion specialist to help guide your students through these routines while you're working with the winds, that's OK. Here are some ideas on how to keep things productive while using the *FMD* program.

- **Have a local university percussion major come in** as an intern to work *FMD* with your students.
- **Assign a student leader** who can corral the percussionists and lead them through the *FMD* routines.
- **Leave wind students with a rotating group of student conductors** to run them through their fundamentals while you run the percussion students through *FMD* routines for 5 minutes.

TECHNIQUES & TERMINOLOGY AT A GLANCE

Below you will find a list of the most common techniques and concepts covered in ***FIVE MINUTE DRILL*** along with a few brief notes on how to approach them. We recognize that there are many different ways to approach just about everything in the percussion realm. Please consider the following as suggestions and not as a replacement for live instruction from a professional. Hopefully these technique tips will complement the style of your particular method!

PRACTICE PAD

TERM	DESCRIPTION
Set Position How you stand at all times	Stand with feet a shoulder width apart with feet angled outward. Have tall posture with relaxed shoulders and a set grip with sticks in the up or down position. Elbows should be relaxed with the beads of the sticks in the center of the pad.
Grip How you hold the stick	The thumbs are flat to the stick. The fingers are wrapped around the stick. The hands are flat to the ground. The overall grip should feel relaxed. A slight downward slope of the palm is acceptable. Even though keyboard mallets have a smaller diameter, the grip is virtually the same.
Legato Strokes The most commonly used stroke	The stick moves in a smooth, nonstop motion from the wrist, creating a consistent, full tone. Keep a consistent height, trying to make all the strokes of a given volume look, sound, and feel the same.
Dynamics Different volumes controlled through stroke height	Get softer by playing lower; get louder by playing higher, being careful not to overdo it on either side. The only thing changing in your stroke is the height—and nothing else.
Flams One of the most commonly used rudiments	Simply add a grace note (unlifted stroke) slightly before a regular stroke. Focus on the timing between strokes, going for the same "chut" sound every time.
Paradiddles An introduction to diddle rudiments	Follows a simple RLRR/LRLL sticking pattern. Pay attention to the differences in height between the accents and the taps. Playing paradiddles with your hands on different surfaces makes a pretty cool groove!
Timing Patterns Sticking patterns for different rhythm combinations	Develops rhythmic control and sticking pattern consistency. One hand uses a legato stroke (nonstop motion), while the other uses a "down stroke" (stops in the down position after striking).

TERM	DESCRIPTION
Double Strokes Used in diddle rudiments (paradiddles, rolls, etc.)	Use the natural rebound of the stick to create a strong second stroke. Relax the back fingers by creating space between the stick and the palm—NEVER the stick and the fingers! Using a little arm at faster speeds is natural and acceptable.
Buzz Strokes Also known as "multiple bounce" strokes	Relax the back fingers with more pressure on the middle finger, using slightly more arm. Keep the stick flat to the drum and try to make the "buzz" sound last until the next stroke. Too much wrist will make the attack too heavy.
Accent/Tap Series of accented and unaccented notes	This means using a combination of *down strokes* (starting high, ending low), *up strokes* (starting low, ending high), and *tap strokes* (low, unaccented strokes). Pay close attention to the strokes just before and after the accents.

KEY BOARD

TERM	DESCRIPTION
Set Position How you stand at all times	Stand far enough forward/back so the mallethead strikes the center of the bar. A common stroke for mallet players is calle the *piston stroke,* which begins in the "up" position at the appropriate height for the volume being played. Strike the bar and return to the up position. Let the back three fingers counterbalance the thumb and forefinger. The best pivot point is usually around the bottom third of the mallet.
Target Zones The optimal point of contact for sound production	Keyboards sound best when struck in the center of the bar over the resonator. In order to keep your range of motion to a minimum, switch to the edge of the bar on sharps/flats as tempos increase. Pay close attention to avoiding the "nodal points" (where the rope goes through the bar).
Circle of 4ths The order in which the scales are presented	This means each scale is an interval of a perfect fourth away from the next scale, either adding a flat or taking away a sharp. This also means that the fourth note of each scale becomes the first note of the next scale.
Major Scales The most common form of scale patterns	Major scales all have the same sequence of whole steps (W) and half steps (H), as in W-W-H-W-W-W-H. Other types of scales (minor, modes, blues) are much easier to play when you know your majors because you can see how they relate to each other.
Chromatic Scales Scales containing every note in the octave	The chromatic scale consists of the smallest building block in western tonal music—the half step. This will help you become more comfortable getting around the entire instrument and at reading naturals and accidentals.

PRACTICE PAD

Breakdown Exercises

Time to roll up the shirt sleeves and get going on the daily practice pad breakdown drills. These drills isolate the basic concepts that will ultimately comprise the Five Minute Drill on page 18. We recommend practicing these exercises *first* as you work toward the full sequence. Be sure to use the tracks on your CD-ROM to keep accurate tempo and to make things more fun!

Here is a brief overview of the practice pad exercises:

1. Legato Strokes & Dynamics
2. Flams & Paradiddles
3. Timing Patterns
4. Double Strokes
5. Buzz Strokes & Accent/Tap
6. Chicken and a Roll
7. Time to Jam!

Remember to record your progress using the Data Tracking Tool PDFs (see page 45) on your CD.

Legato Strokes & Dynamics

QUICK TIPS

Legato Strokes
- Consistent heights and grip
- Relaxed, smooth motion from the wrist
- Back fingers on stick
- Hand at rest stays set
- Mostly wrist with a little arm

Dynamics
- Consistent heights and grip
- Relaxed, smooth motion from the wrist
- Don't slow down or speed up
- Be patient and gradual when changing heights for a crescendo or decrescendo

Play-along Tracks
01 - SLOW – 84 bpm (01'47")
02 - MEDIUM – 100 bpm (01'30")
03 - FAST – 116 bpm (01'18")

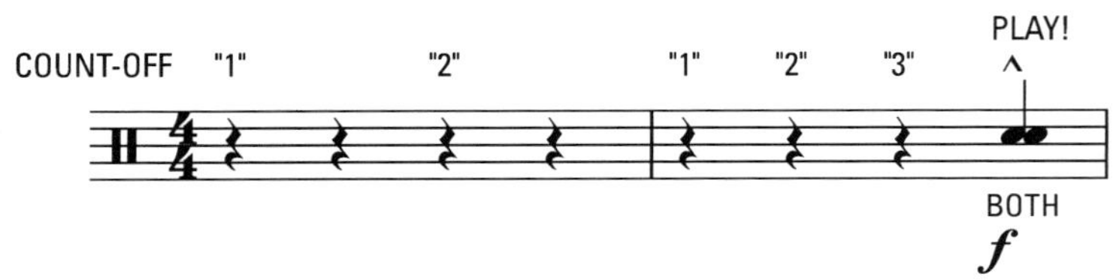

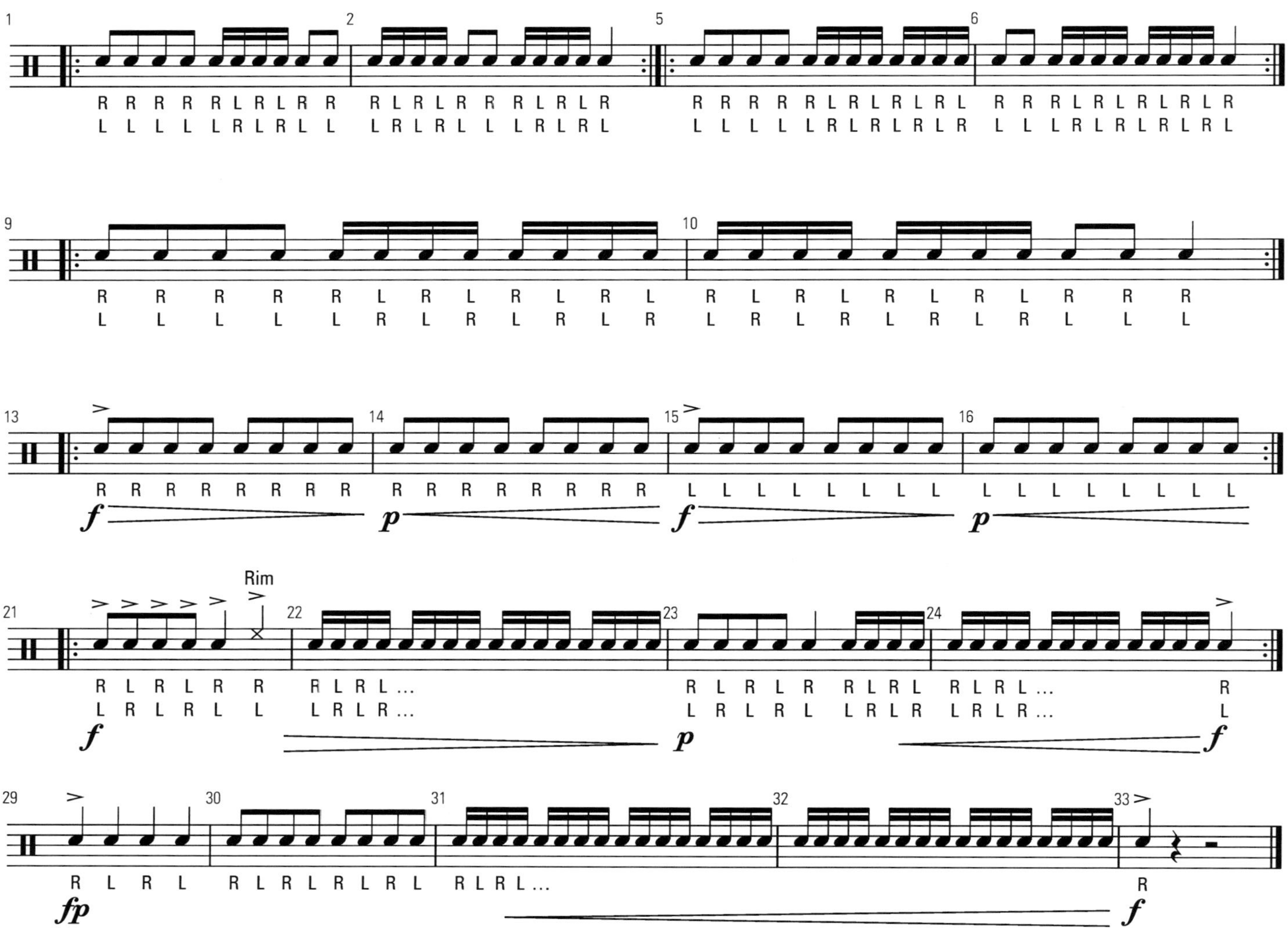

Flams & Paradiddles

QUICK TIPS

Flams
- Consistent heights and grip
- Should sound like "chut"
- Pay attention to *Down/Up/Tap* strokes
- Don't slow down or speed up
- Upper case R's and L's indicate high notes; lower case r's and l's indicate low notes

Paradiddles
- Consistent heights and grip
- Use Down strokes after the accents
- Control the bounce of the "diddle" strokes
- Be patient and careful not to rush
- Upper case R's and L's indicate high notes; lower case r's and l's indicate low notes

Play-along Tracks
04 - SLOW – 120 bpm (01'21")
05 - MEDIUM – 140 bpm (01'10")
06 - FAST – 160 bpm (01'01")

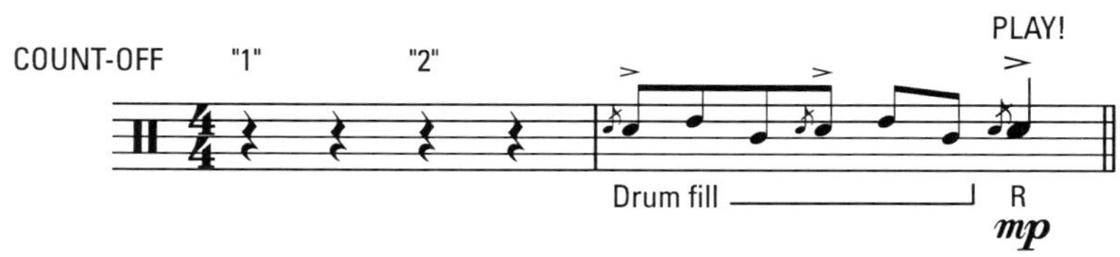

Timing Patterns

QUICK TIPS

- Consistent heights and grip
- Pay attention to different stroke types—legato vs. controlled
- Line up with the groove!

Play-along Tracks

07 - SLOW – 85 bpm (00'58")
08 - MEDIUM – 95 bpm (00'52")
09 - FAST – 105 bpm (00'47")

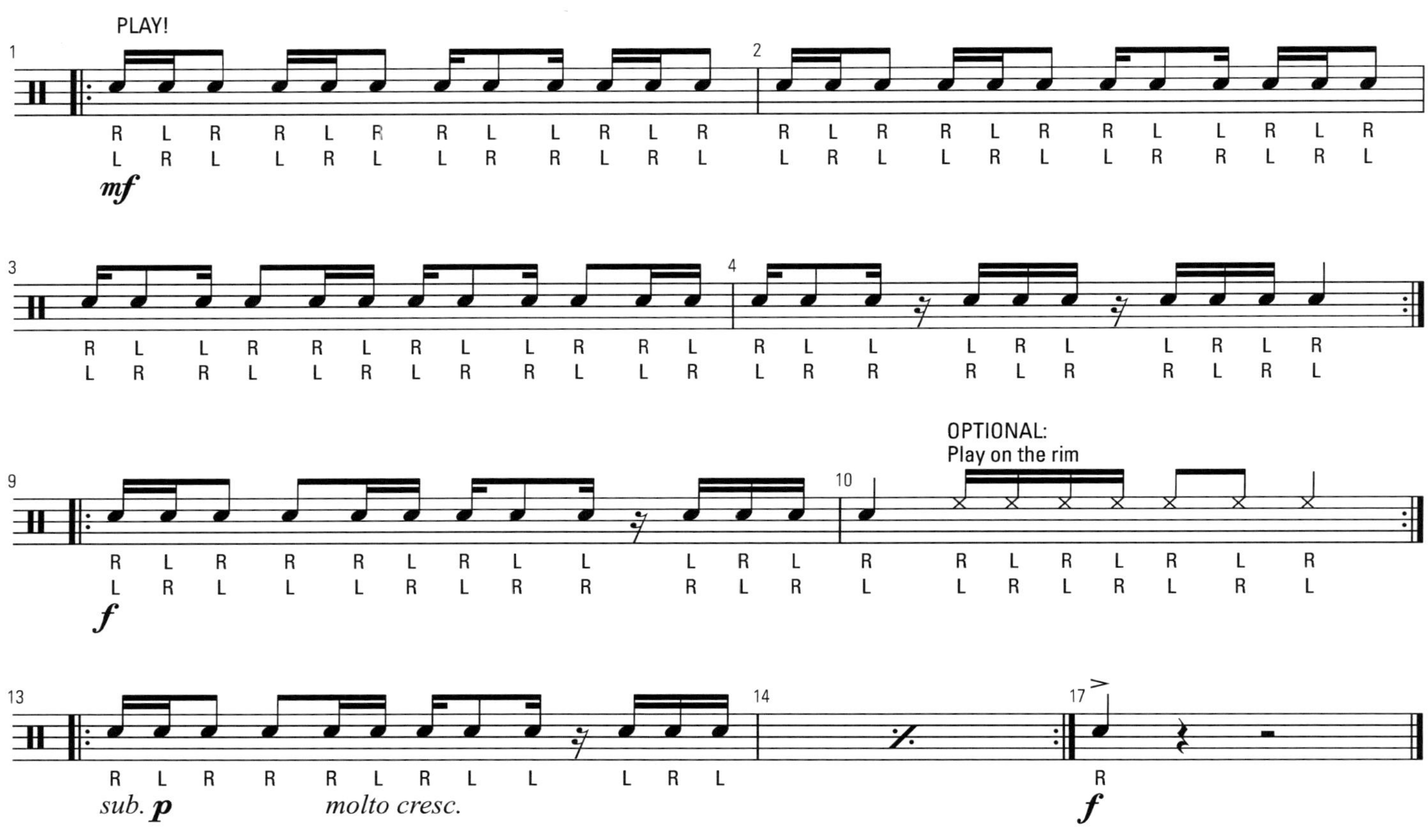

Double Strokes

QUICK TIPS

- Consistent heights and grip
- Use back fingers to control the second stroke of each double
- Space between stick and palm but not between stick and finger

Play-along Tracks

10 - SLOW – 76 bpm (00'50")
11 - MEDIUM – 86 bpm (00'44")
12 - FAST – 96 bpm (00'39")

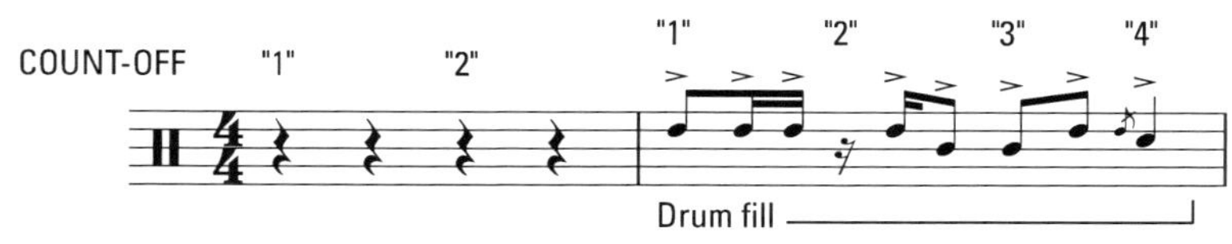

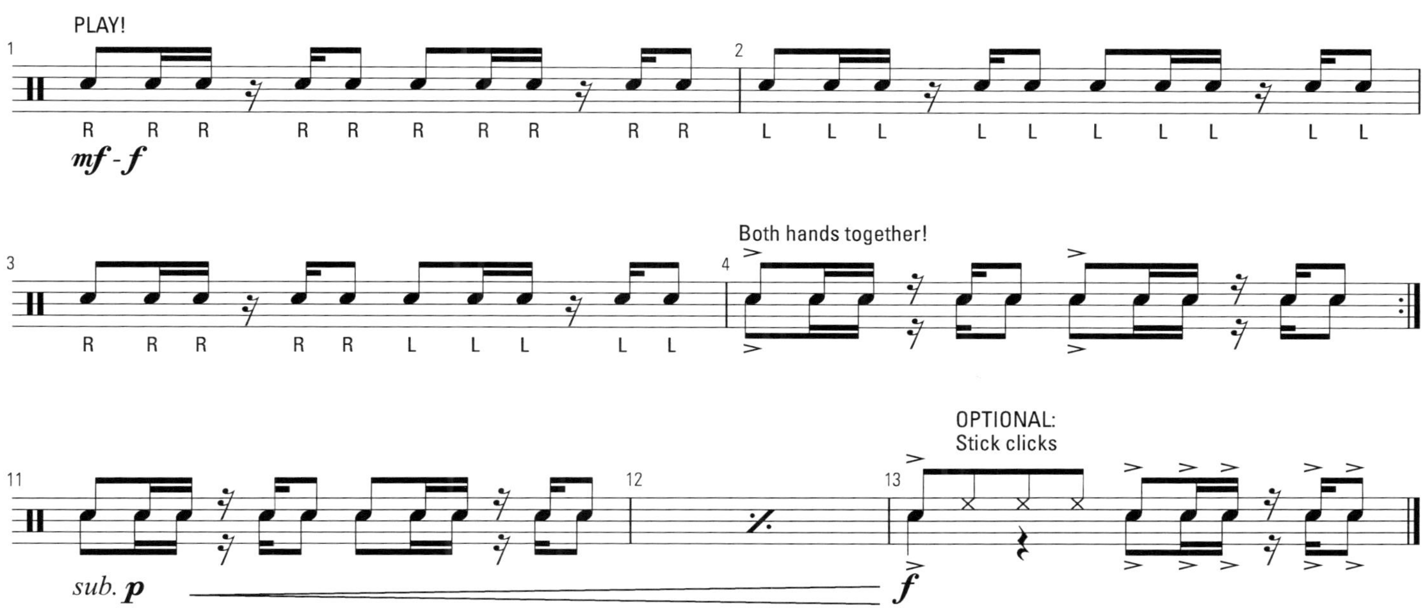

Buzz Strokes & Accent/Tap

QUICK TIPS

Buzz Strokes
- Consistent heights and grip
- Relax back fingers
- More pressure on middle finger
- Keep the stick flat to the drum
- Upper case R's and L's indicate high notes; lower case r's and l's indicate low notes

Accent/Tap
- Consistent heights and grip
- Pay attention to *Down/Up/Tap* strokes
- Pay attention to the taps before and after each accent
- Upper case R's and L's indicate high notes; lower case r's and l's indicate low notes

Play-along Tracks

13 - SLOW – 84 bpm (00'59")
14 - MEDIUM – 94 bpm (00'54")
15 - FAST – 104 bpm (00'49")

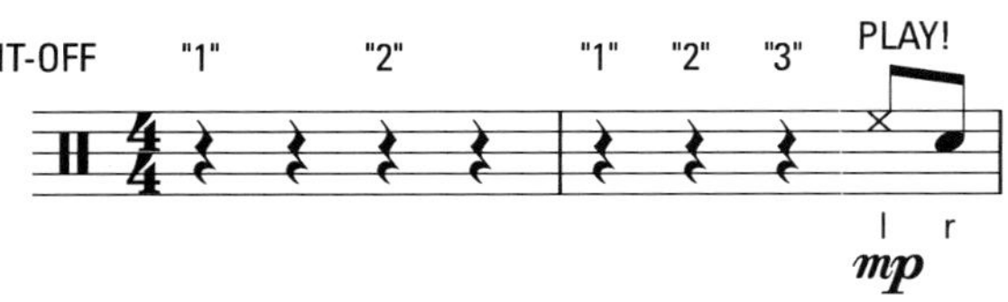

Chicken and a Roll

QUICK TIPS

- Consistent heights and grip
- Make the buzzes "touch"
- Find the pulse in the recording
- Keep the stick flat to the drum
- Also try using "double strokes" rather than buzz strokes

Play-along Tracks

16 - SLOW – 70-155 bpm (00'52")
17 - MEDIUM – 70-175 bpm (00'48")
18 - FAST – 70-225 bpm (00'42")

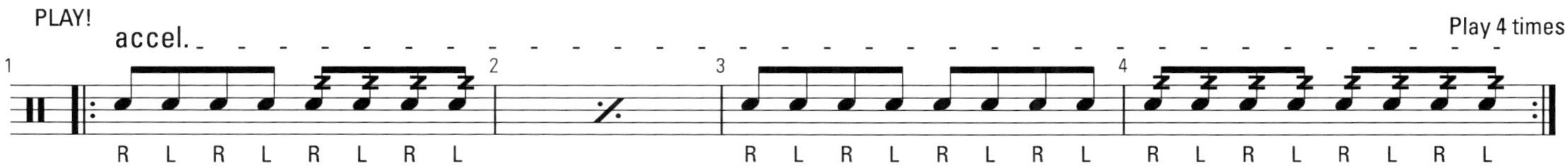

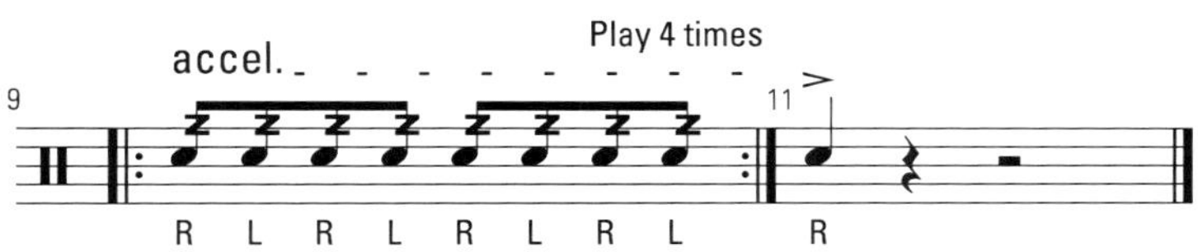

Time to Jam!

QUICK TIPS

- Consistent heights and grip
- Don't get too excited!
- Have fun WHILE STAYING FOCUSED

Play-along Tracks

19 - SLOW – 140 bpm (00'29")
20 - MEDIUM – 155 bpm (00'26")
21 - FAST – 170 bpm (00'24")

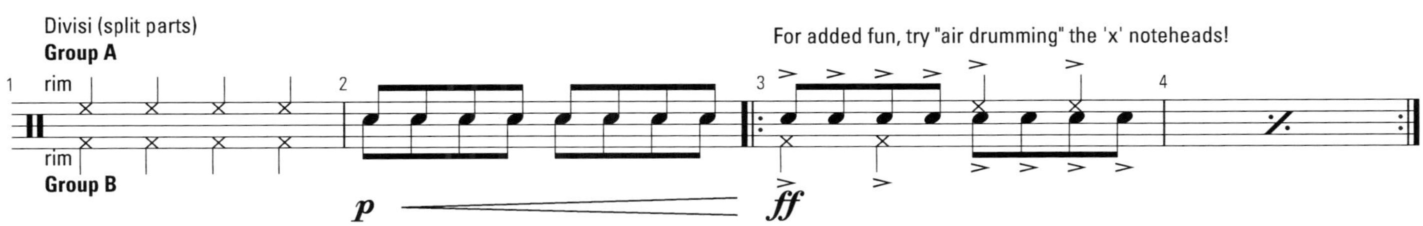

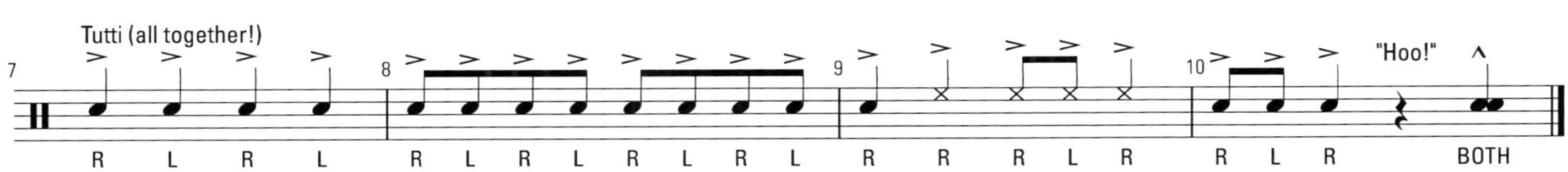

Play-along Tracks
22 - **SLOW** (06'50")
23 - **MEDIUM** (06'00")
24 - **FAST** (05'18")

PRACTICE PAD
Full Sequence

Legato Strokes & Dynamics

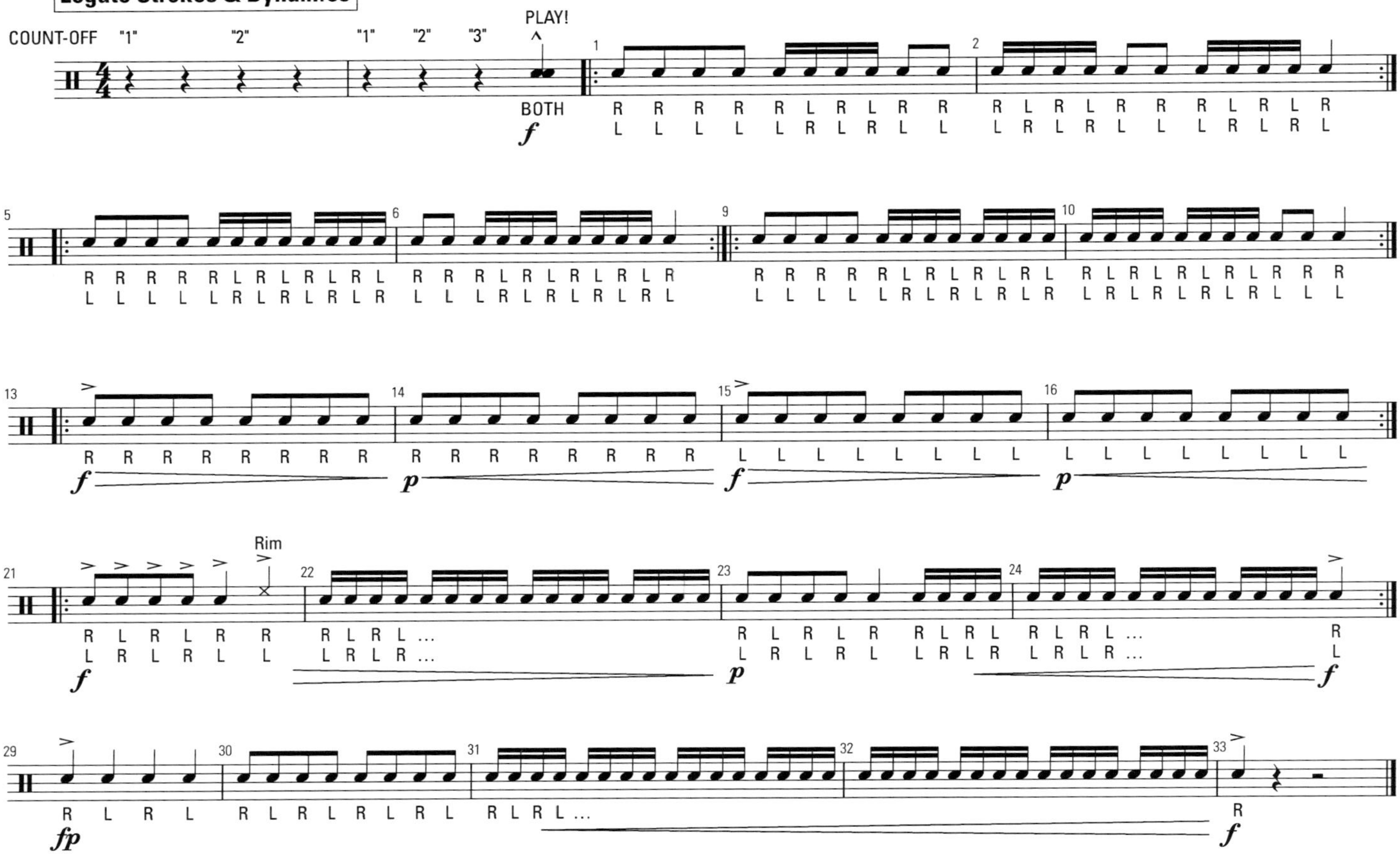

Flams & Paradiddles

Timing Patterns

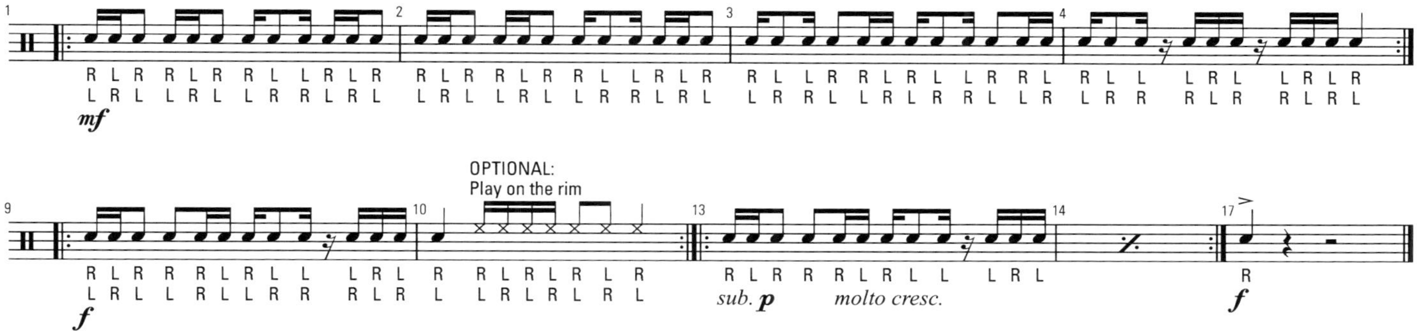

Double Strokes

Buzz Strokes & Accent/Tap

Chicken & a Roll

Time to Jam!

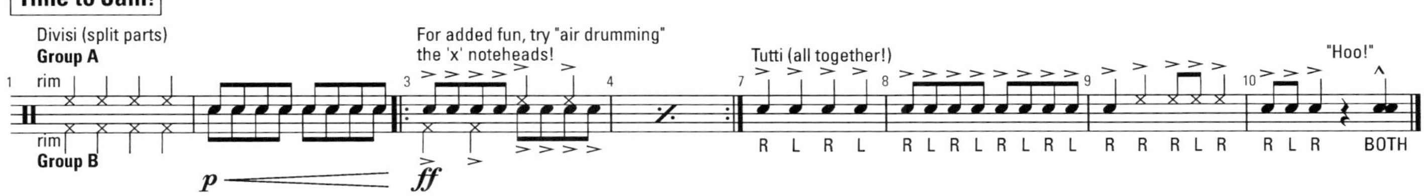

KEYBOARD

Major Scale Breakdown Exercises

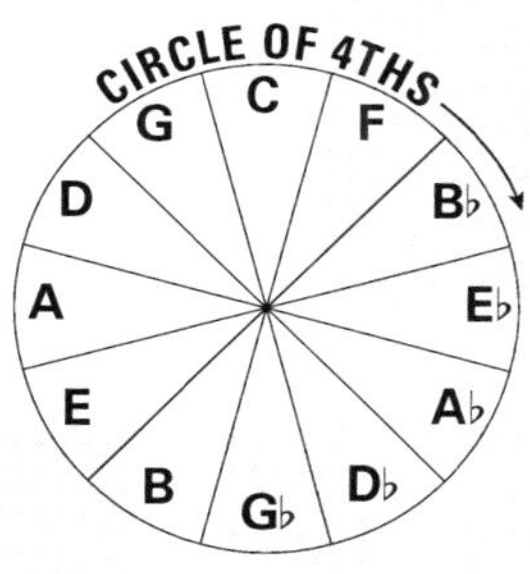

This next section serves as an introduction to all twelve major diatonic scales. Using the Circle of 4ths *(left)*, we will start with the basic key of C Major and proceed around in clockwise fashion until all twelve major keys have been covered. The exercises work each scale in both stepwise motion and in an arpeggiated fashion. Using the tracks on your CD-ROM, work each scale until you have mastered it and then move to the next.

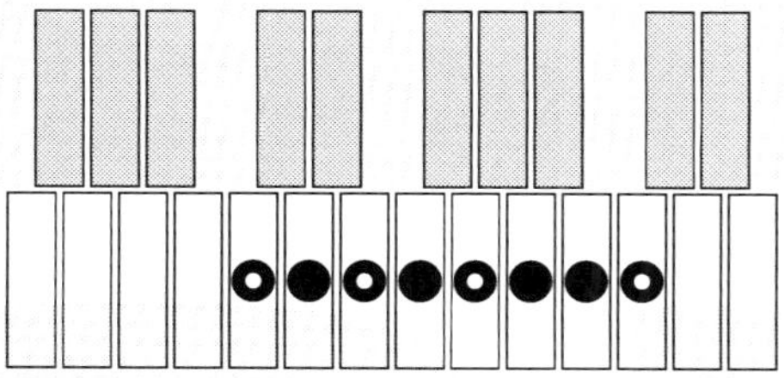

Use the small, two-octave keyboard diagram at the top of each page as a reference point for which bars to strike for that particular scale. White dots illustrate the arpeggio.

GENERAL TECHNIQUE TIPS

- Keep mallet heights and grip consistent.
- The motions and strokes you make should be consistent.
- Stay off the nodes (the part where the string goes through the bar).
- Notice the shape the scale makes.

C Major

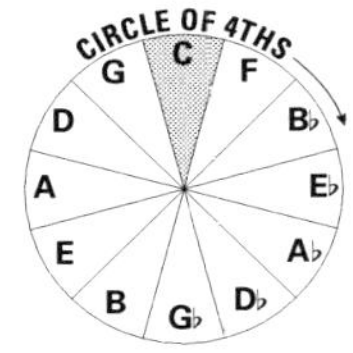

No Flats / No Sharps

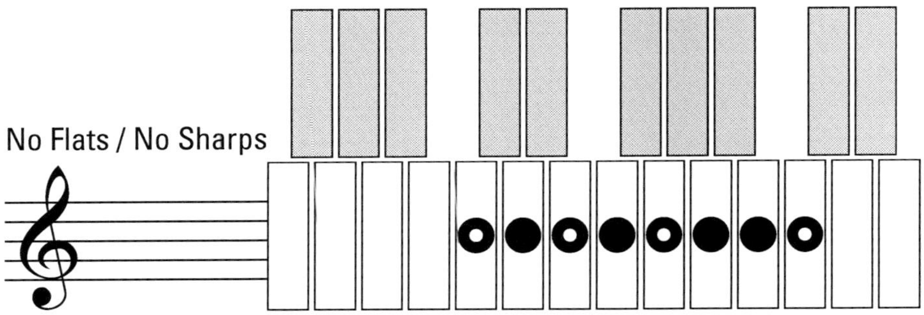

TIP of the DAY

Be sure to use a relaxed legato stroke. A fluid motion goes a long way!

Play-along Tracks

25 - SLOW – 92 bpm (01'47")
26 - MEDIUM – 104 bpm (01'35")
27 - FAST – 116 bpm (01'25")

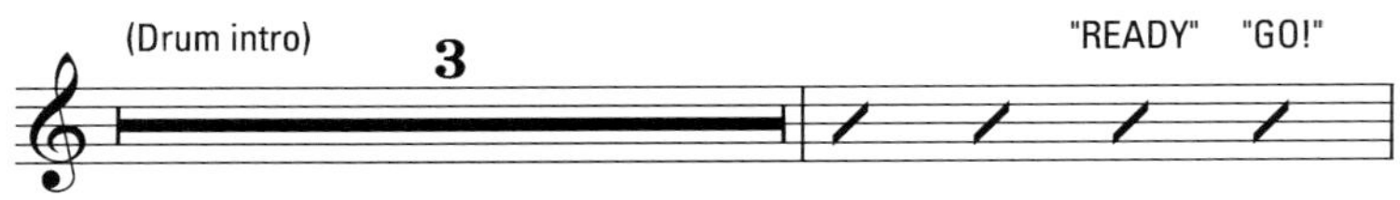

FOUR-NOTE

TWO-NOTE

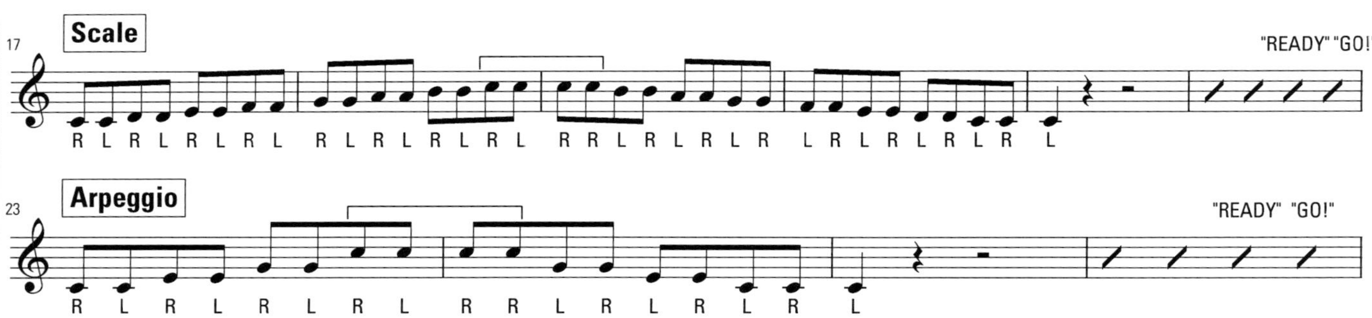

ONE-NOTE

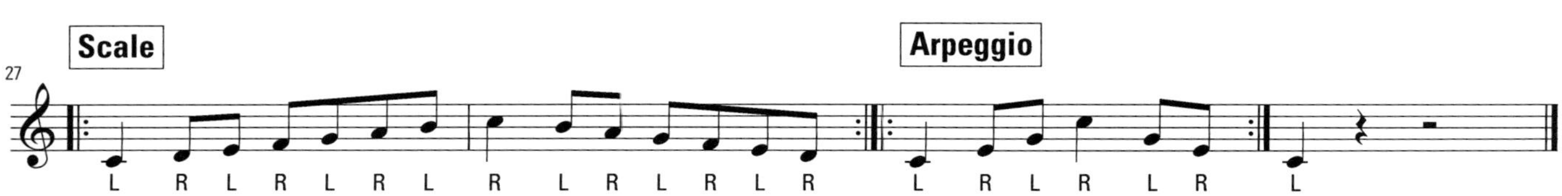

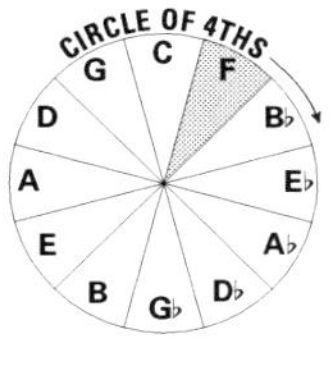

F Major

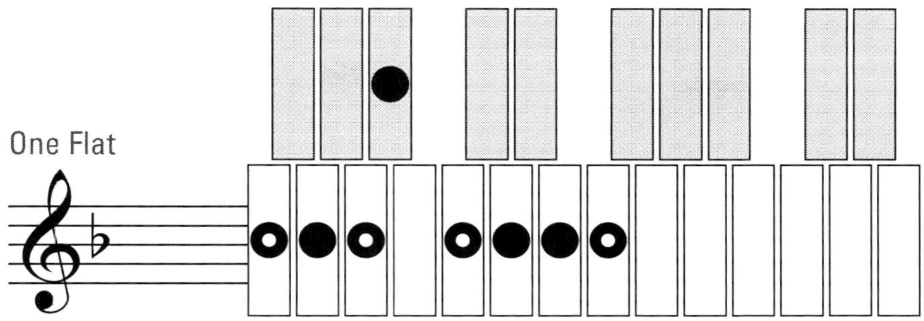

TIP of the DAY

If you use a big mallet height, you will build "muscle memory" more quickly. This will make life easier for you, so feel free to "play out!"

Play-along Tracks

28 - SLOW – 92 bpm (01'47")
29 - MEDIUM – 104 bpm (01'35")
30 - FAST – 116 bpm (01'25")

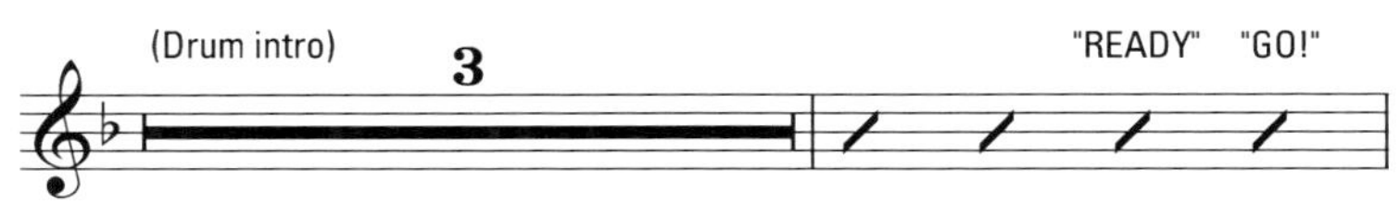

FOUR-NOTE

TWO-NOTE

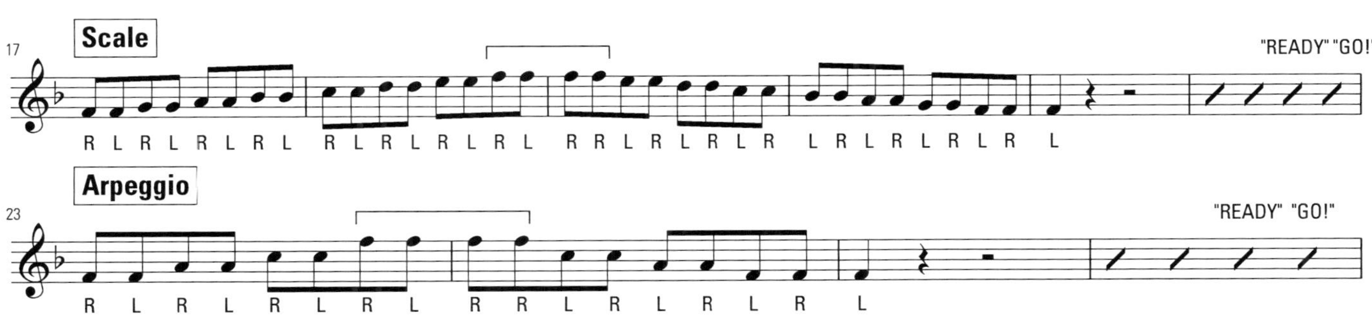

ONE-NOTE

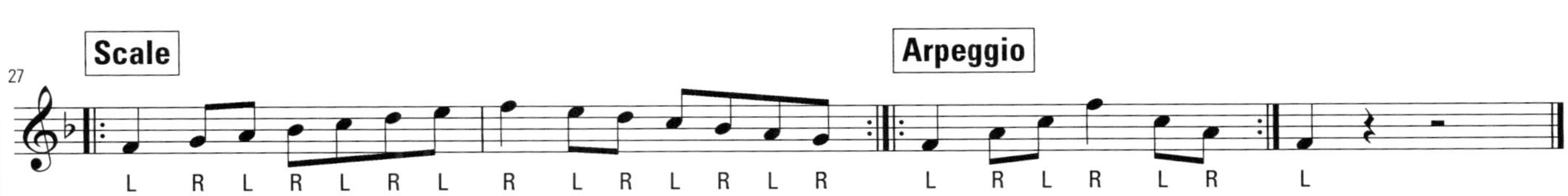

B♭ Major

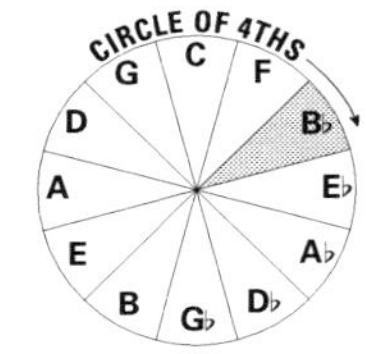

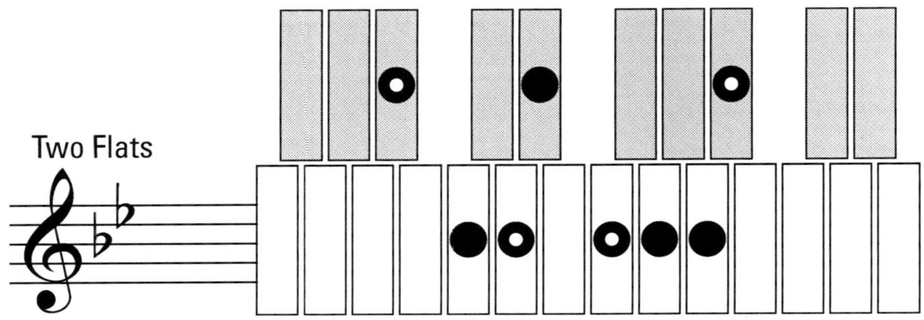

TIP of the DAY

As you start playing more flats or sharps (black keys on the piano), be sure you are playing in the center of the bars for these notes, too!

Play-along Tracks

31 - SLOW – 92 bpm (01'47")
32 - MEDIUM – 104 bpm (01'35")
33 - FAST – 116 bpm (01'25")

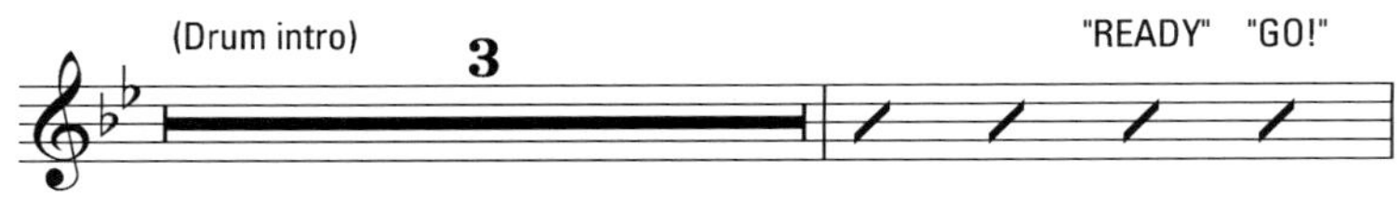

FOUR-NOTE

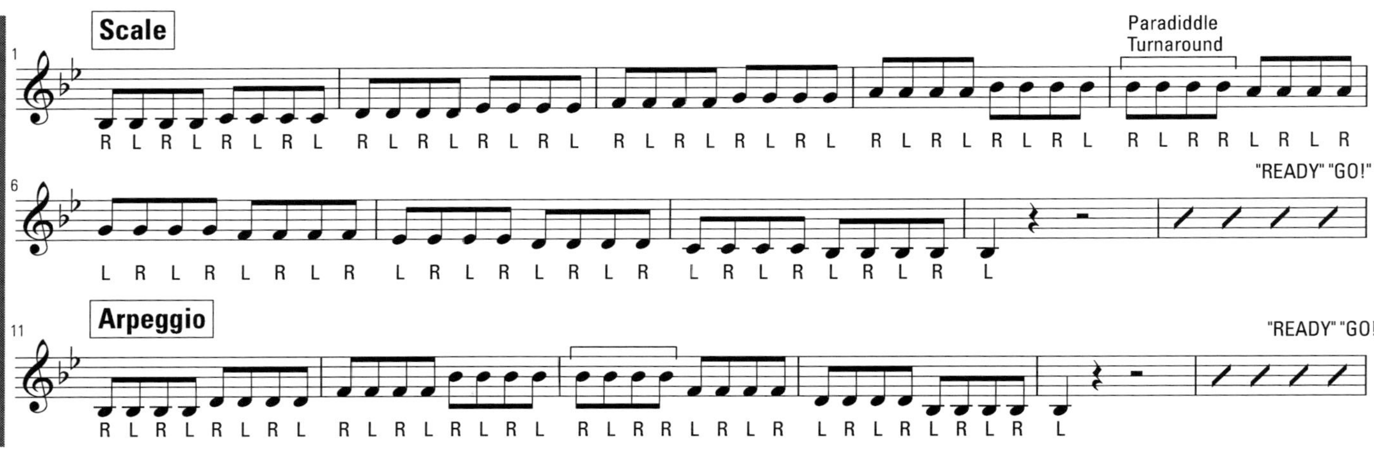

TWO-NOTE

ONE-NOTE

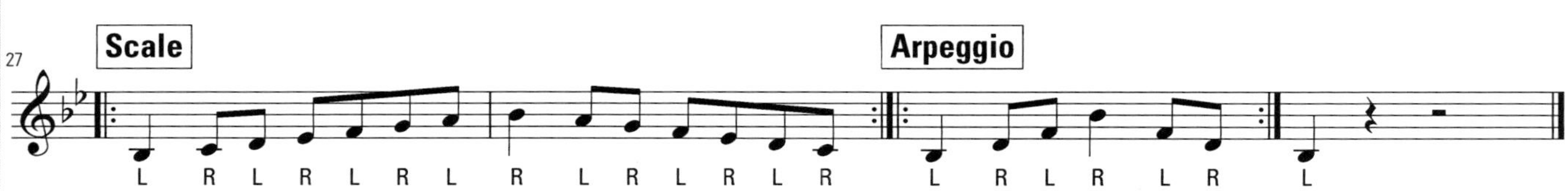

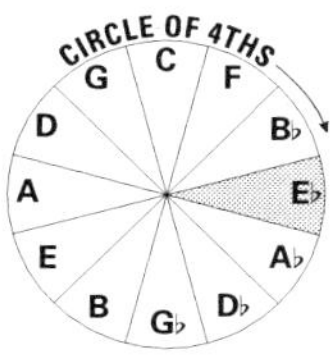

E♭ Major

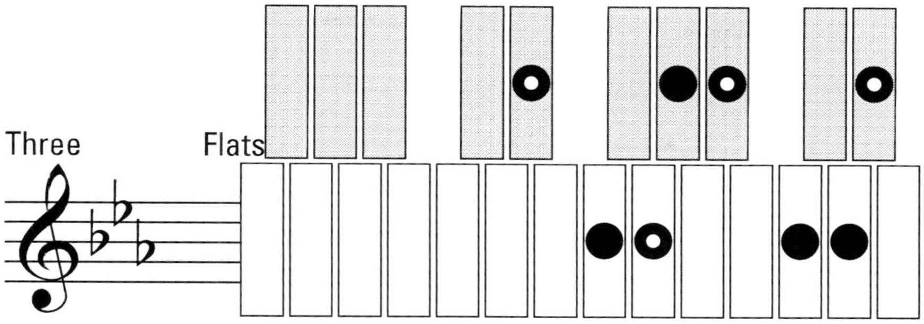

TIP of the DAY

Scales that use a mixture of naturals (white keys) and accidentals (black keys) can begin to get in the way of an efficient stroke. Make sure you are continuing to use a fluid motion.

Play-along Tracks

34 - SLOW – 92 bpm (01'47")
35 - MEDIUM – 104 bpm (01'35")
36 - FAST – 116 bpm (01'25")

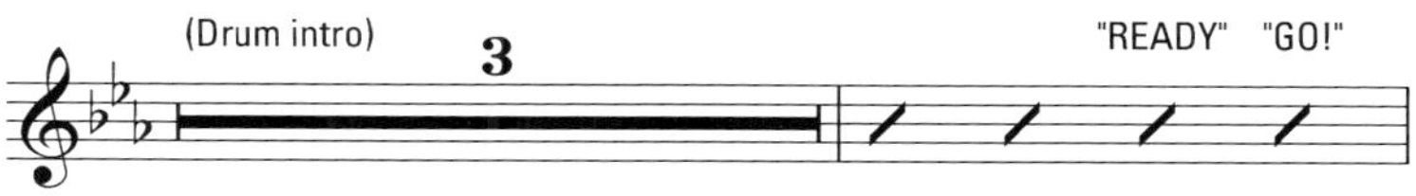

FOUR-NOTE

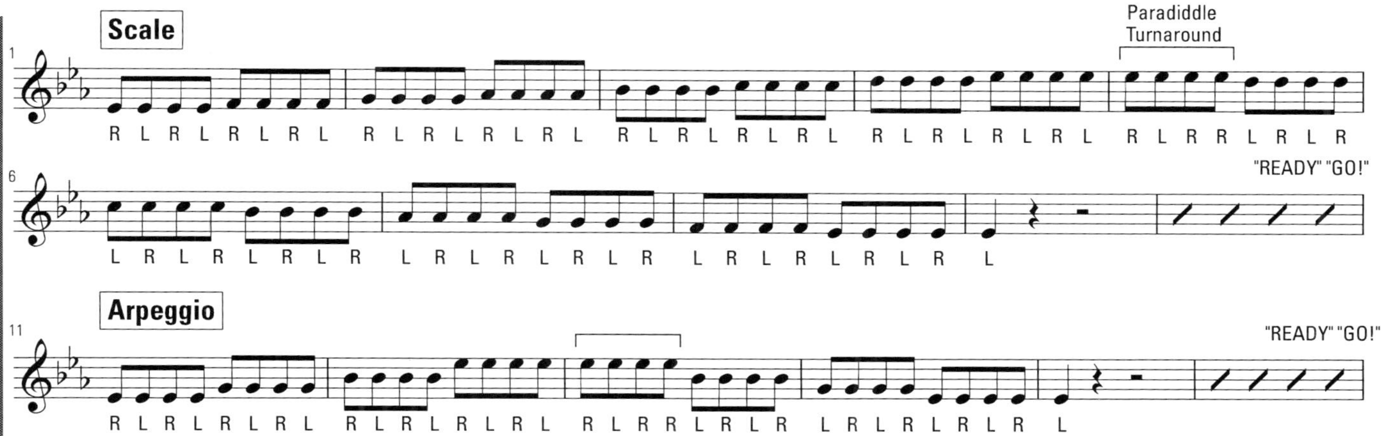

TWO-NOTE

ONE-NOTE

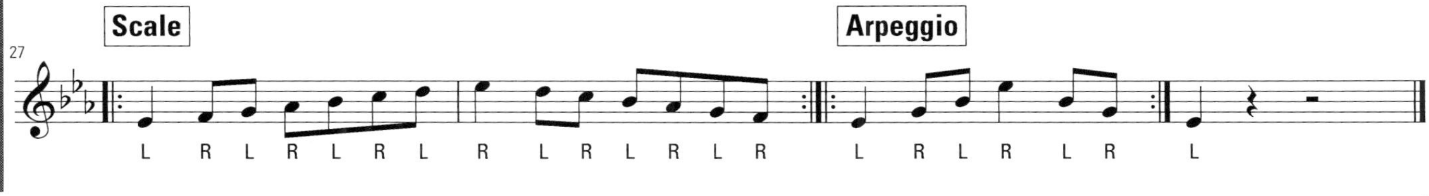

A♭ Major

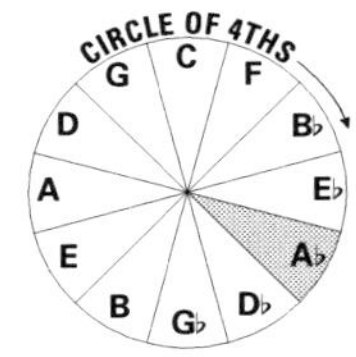

Four Flats

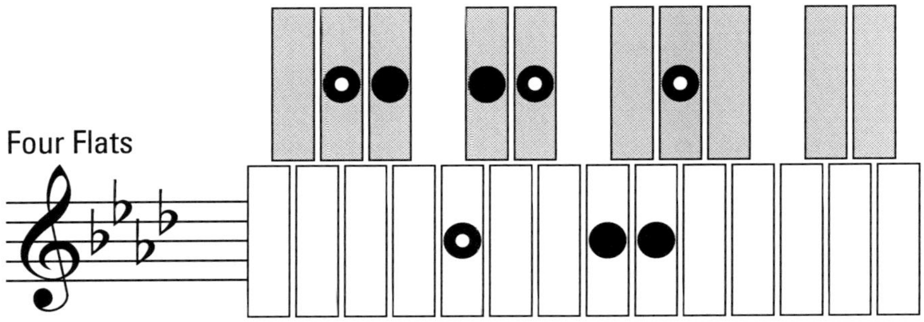

TIP of the DAY

Try using the motion after you strike the bar to move the mallet toward its next note. In other words, think horizontally and vertically.

Play-along Tracks

37 - SLOW – 92 bpm (01'47")
38 - MEDIUM – 104 bpm (01'35")
39 - FAST – 116 bpm (01'25")

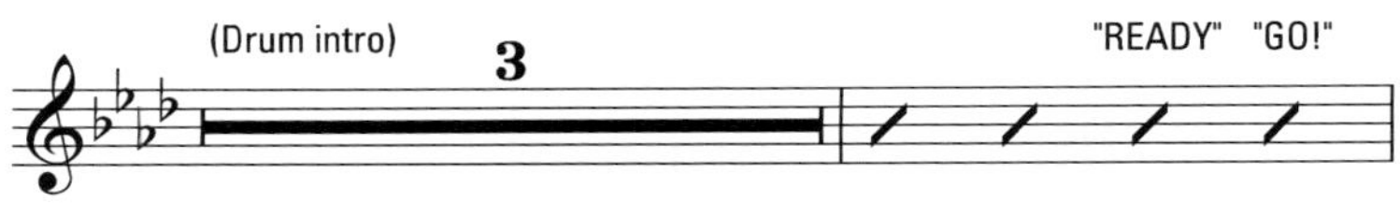

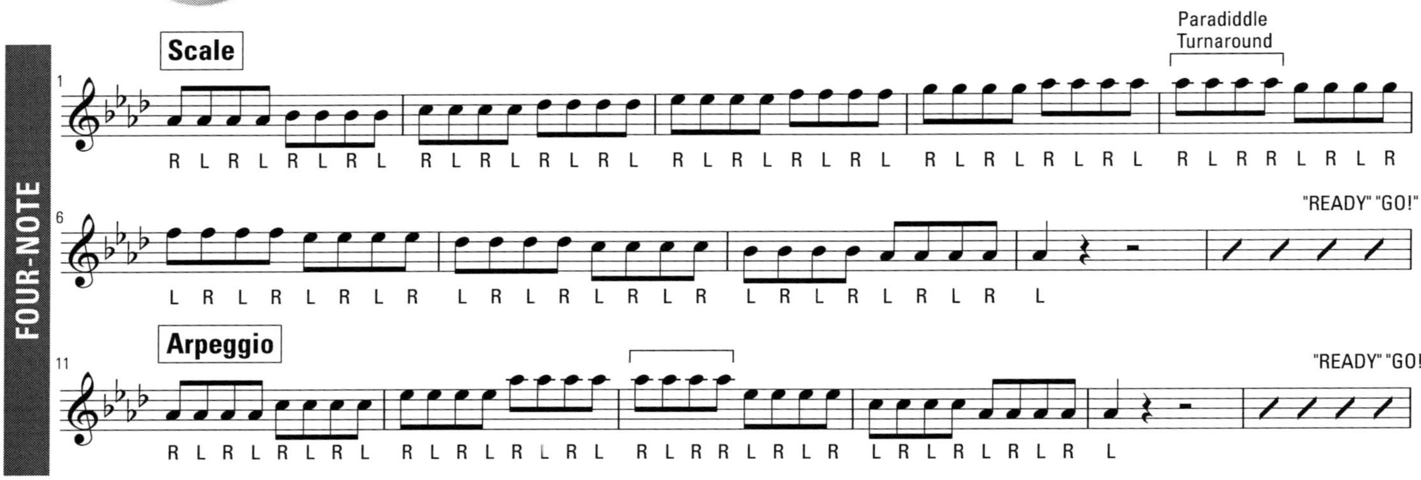

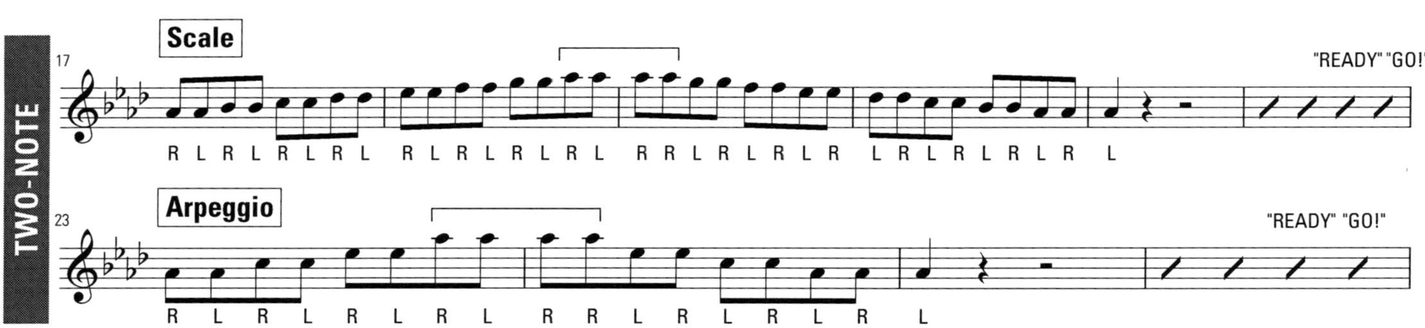

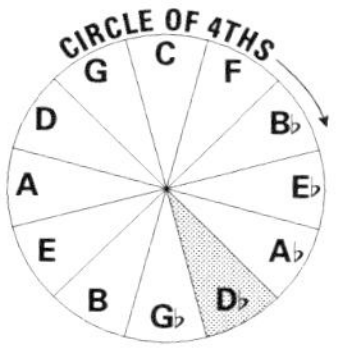

D♭ Major

Five Flats

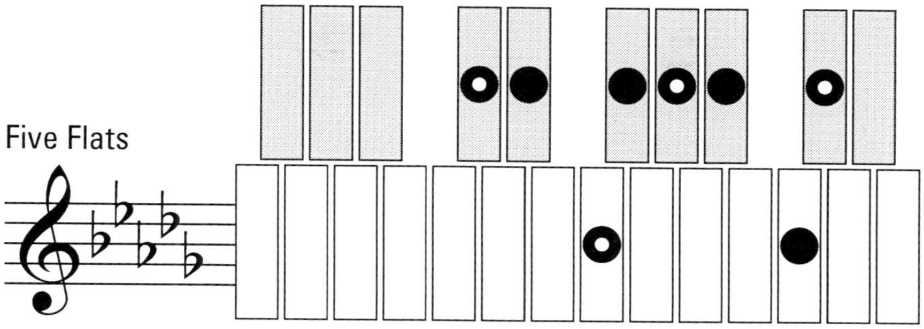

TIP of the DAY

Are you getting the same quality of sound out of all your notes?
Are you hitting each bar with the same velocity and energy?

Play-along Tracks

40 - SLOW – 92 bpm (01'47")
41 - MEDIUM – 104 bpm (01'35")
42 - FAST – 116 bpm (01'25")

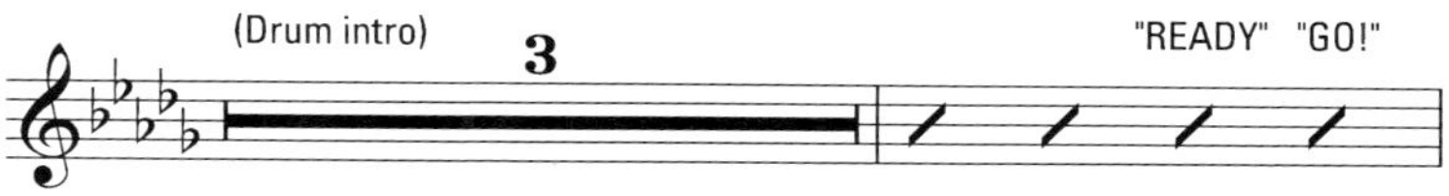

FOUR-NOTE

Scale

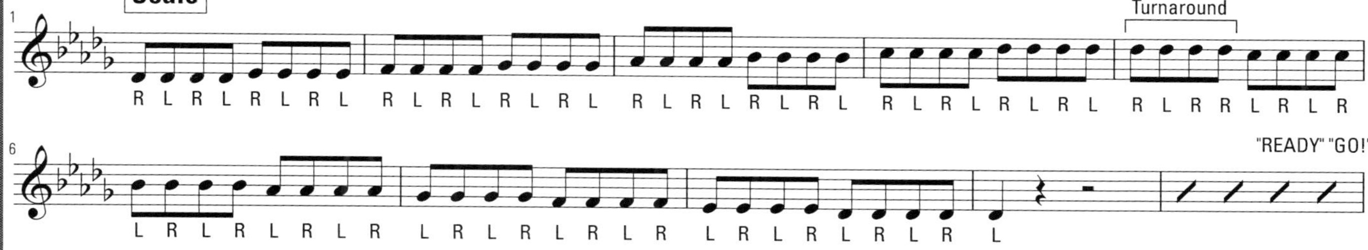

Arpeggio

TWO-NOTE

Scale

Arpeggio

ONE-NOTE

Scale **Arpeggio**

G♭ Major

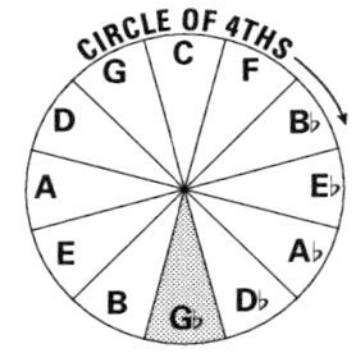

Six Flats

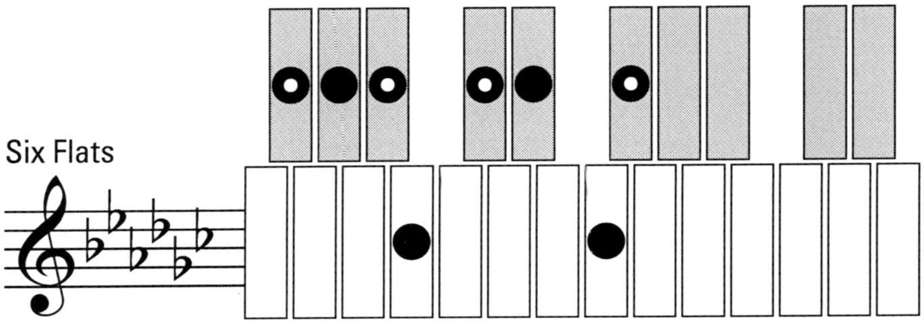

TIP of the DAY

Take note of whether you are using an extra motion when you play (e.g., prep strokes or bouncing during the rebound). Use only the minimum amount of motion to efficiently strike the bar.

Play-along Tracks

43 - SLOW – 92 bpm (01'47")
44 - MEDIUM – 104 bpm (01'35")
45 - FAST – 116 bpm (01'25")

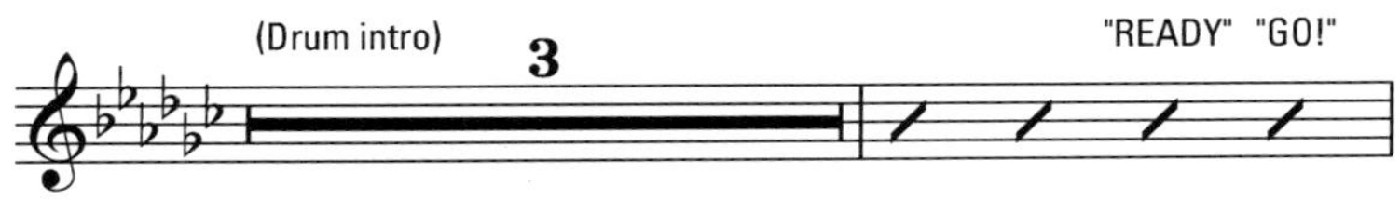

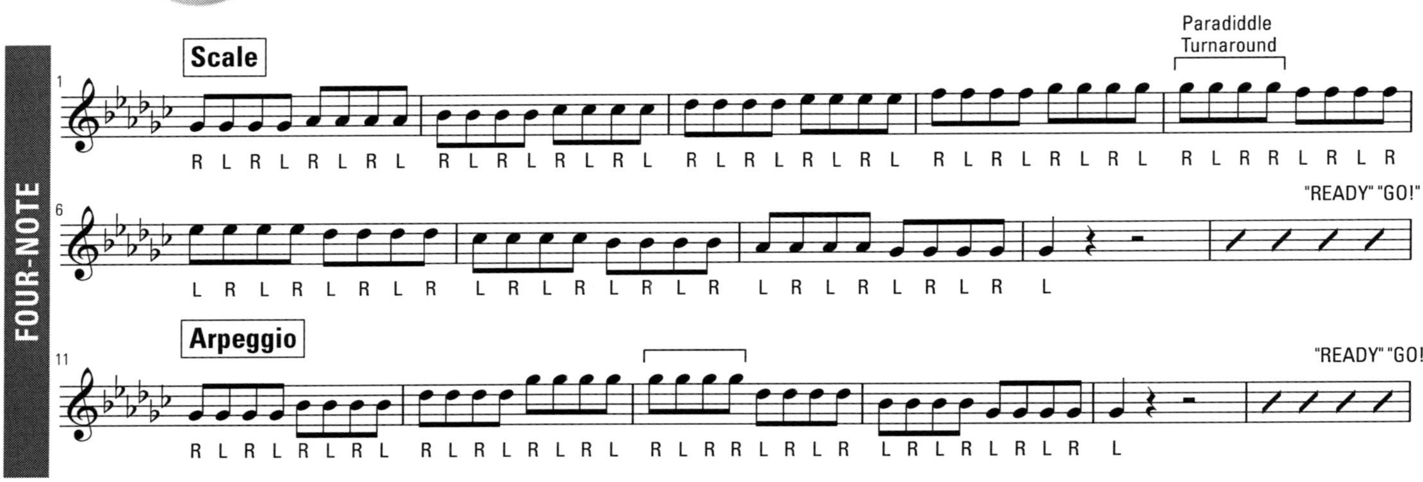

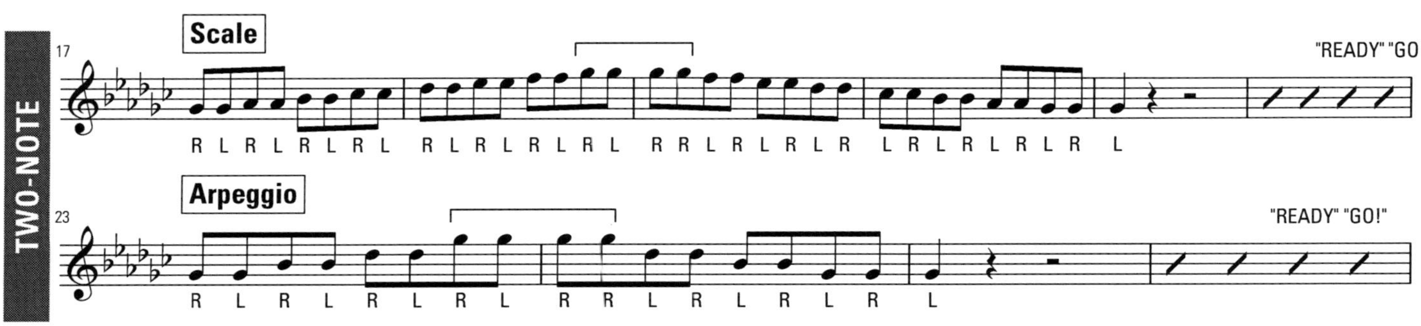

B Major

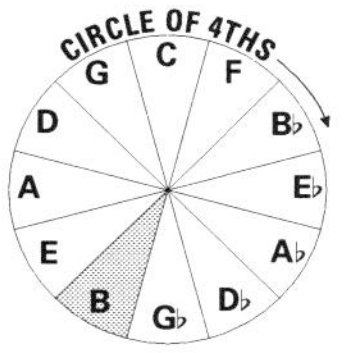

Five Sharps

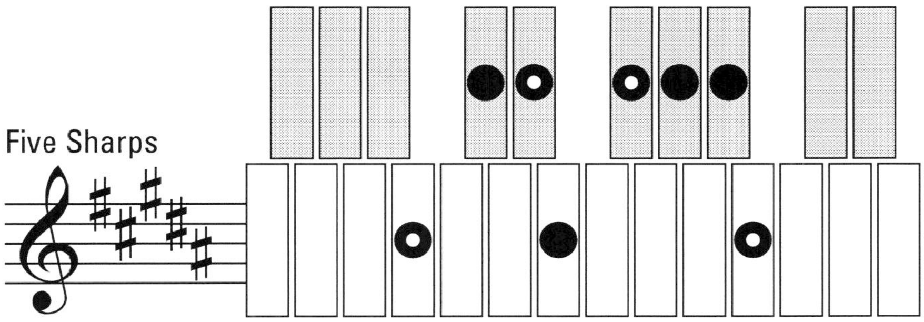

TIP of the DAY

Be sure to keep your stick heights equal to achieve an equal volume. When you strike an accidental, be sure the note doesn't "pop out" or sound too soft.

Play-along Tracks

46 - SLOW – 92 bpm (01'47")
47 - MEDIUM – 104 bpm (01'35")
48 - FAST – 116 bpm (01'25")

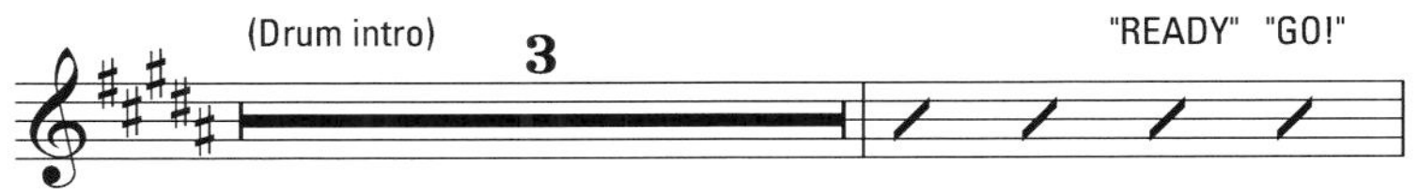

FOUR-NOTE

Scale

Arpeggio

TWO-NOTE

Scale

Arpeggio

ONE-NOTE

Scale **Arpeggio**

E Major

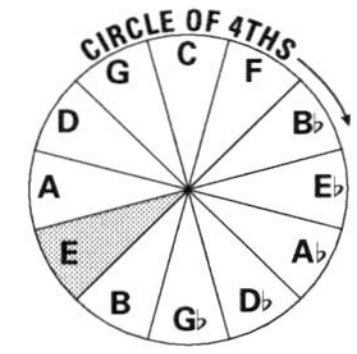

Four Sharps

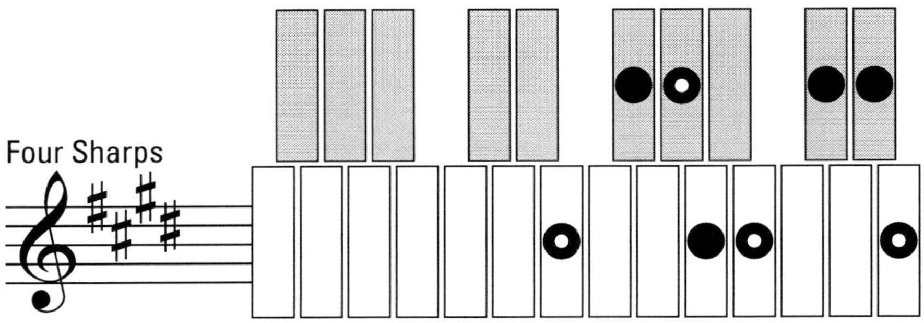

TIP of the DAY

When you feel comfortable with your scales, try playing them dynamically. Crescendo as the scale ascends and decrescendo as the scale descends. (Also try the opposite way!)

Play-along Tracks

49 - SLOW – 92 bpm (01'47")
50 - MEDIUM – 104 bpm (01'35")
51 - FAST – 116 bpm (01'25")

FOUR-NOTE

Scale

Arpeggio

TWO-NOTE

Scale

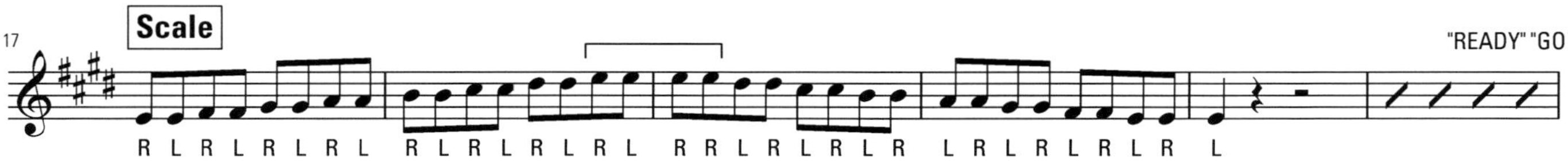

Arpeggio

ONE-NOTE

Scale

Arpeggio

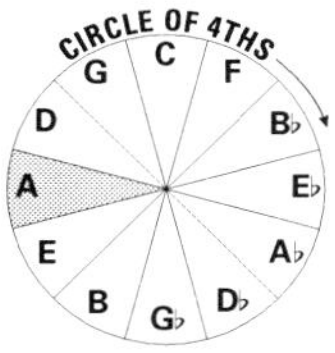

A Major

Three Sharps

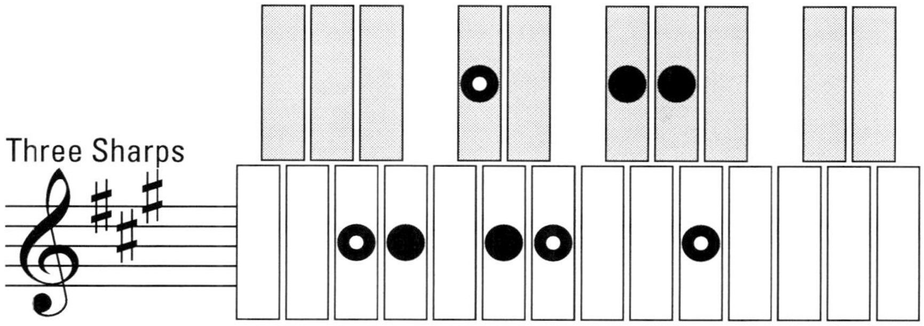

TIP of the DAY

Are you staying relaxed? Are you using only the necessary motion? No matter how advanced the percussionist, the best ones are continually evaluating their motions.

Play-along Tracks

52 - SLOW – 92 bpm (01'47")
53 - MEDIUM – 104 bpm (01'35")
54 - FAST – 116 bpm (01'25")

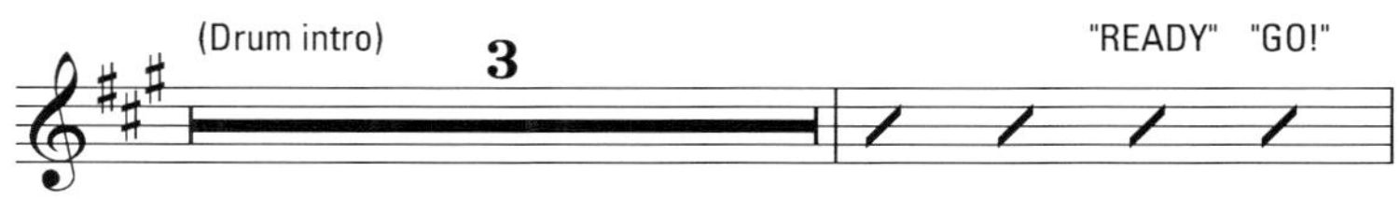

FOUR-NOTE

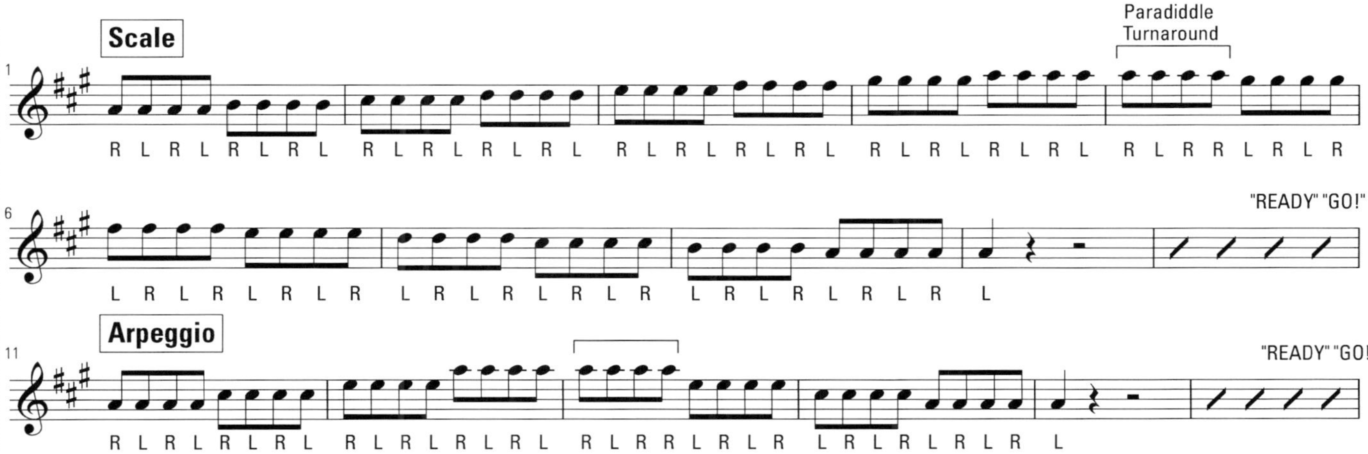

TWO-NOTE

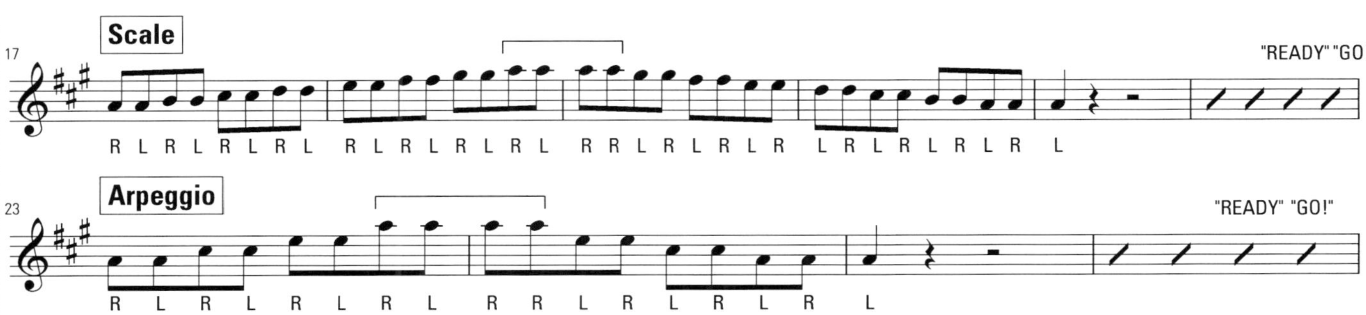

ONE-NOTE

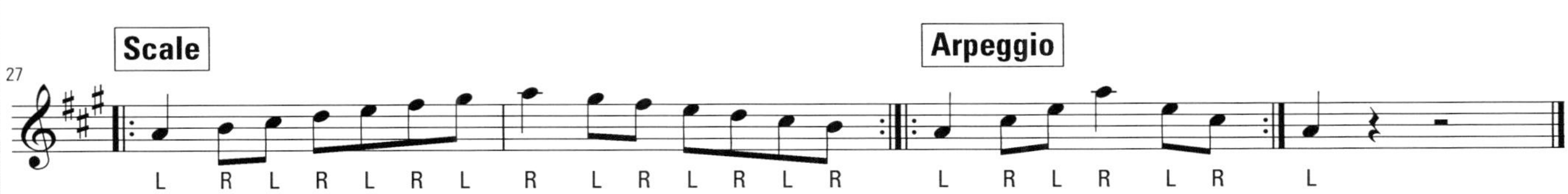

D Major

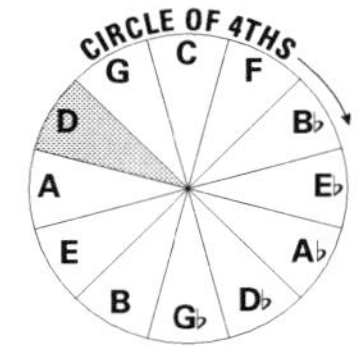

Two Sharps

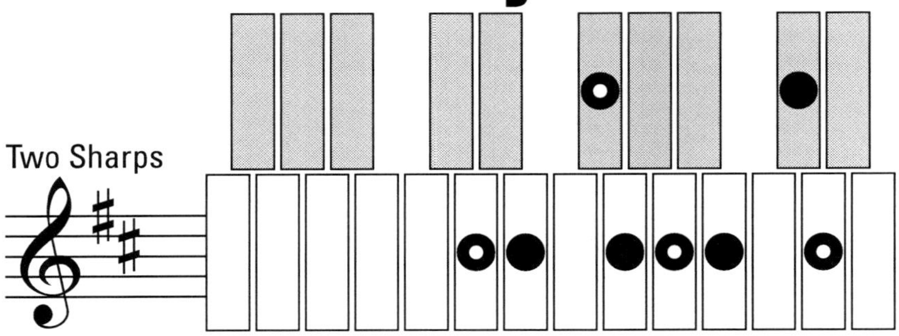

TIP of the DAY

FULCRUM CHECK: Let the point where the index finger and thumb meet on the mallet be the main focal point of your grip, but let your back three fingers help carry some of the weight of the mallet.

Play-along Tracks

55 - SLOW – 92 bpm (01'47")
56 - MEDIUM – 104 bpm (01'35")
57 - FAST – 116 bpm (01'25")

FOUR-NOTE

Scale

Arpeggio

TWO-NOTE

Scale

Arpeggio

ONE-NOTE

Scale **Arpeggio**

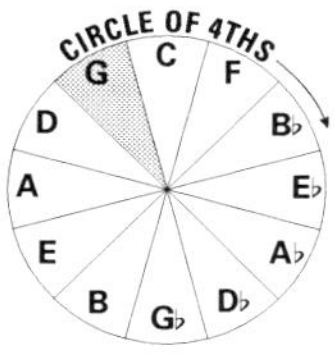

G Major

One Sharp

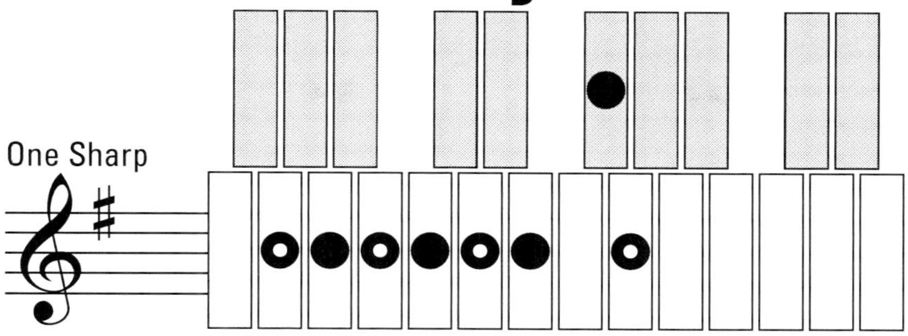

TIP of the DAY

GRIP CHECK!

1. Thumbs are *flat*.
2. Hands are *flat*.
3. Fingers are *wrapped* around the stick.
4. It should feel *relaxed*.

Play-along Tracks

58 - SLOW – 92 bpm (01'47")
59 - MEDIUM – 104 bpm (01'35")
60 - FAST – 116 bpm (01'25")

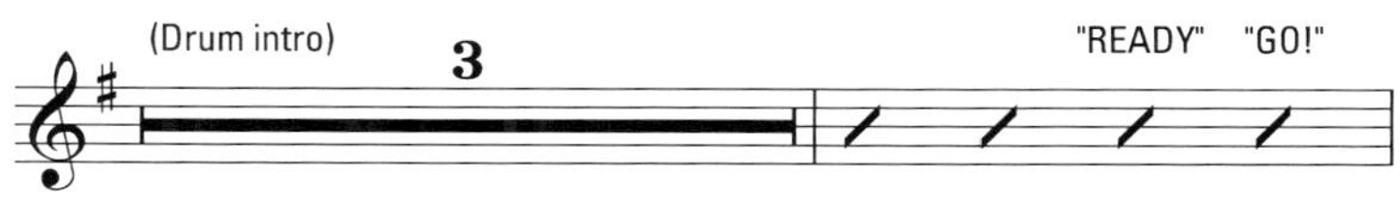

FOUR-NOTE

Scale

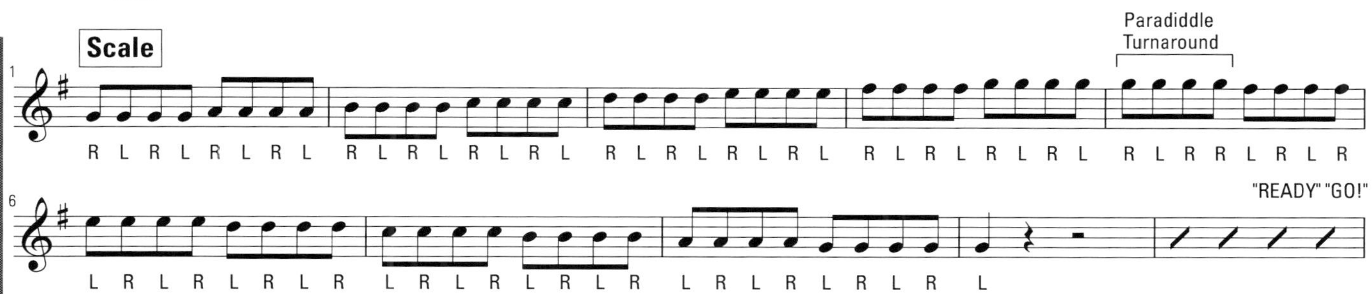

Arpeggio

TWO-NOTE

Scale

Arpeggio

ONE-NOTE

Scale **Arpeggio**

MAJOR SCALES
Full Sequence

Okay. Now that you've mastered the scale breakdowns of the previous section, you're ready to roll into the FULL sequence for all twelve major scales. This sequence is presented with two variations—a one-octave version and a two-octave version—both of which can be played simultaneously. If you're a beginner, start with the top staff (one-octave version). More experienced players may choose to play the two-octave version presented on the lower staff. Note that on the two-octave version, the hand that plays an accidental will *switch* in the second octave!

Play-along Tracks
61 - SLOW – 100 bpm (04'25")
62 - MEDIUM – 112 bpm (04'06")
63 - FAST – 124 bpm (03'40")

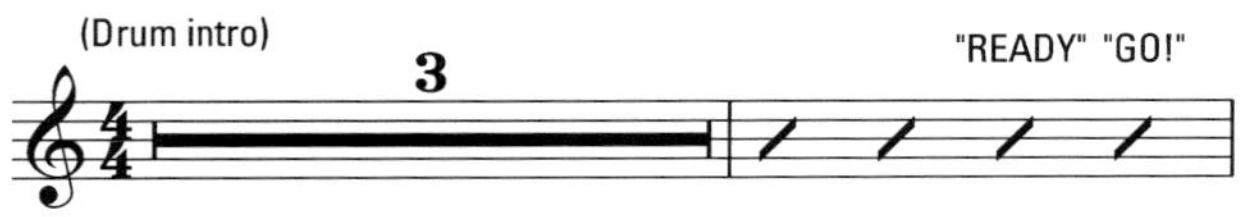

B♭ Major

E♭ Major

A♭ Major

D♭ Major

G♭ Major

B Major

E Major

A Major

D Major

G Major

One Octave
L R L R L R L R L R L R L R L R L R L R L R L R L R L R
Two Octave
L R L R L R L R L R L R L R L R L R L R L R L R L R L R
One
L R L R L R L R L R L R L
Two
L R L R L R L R L R L R L

KEYBOARD

Chromatic Scale Sequences

Here lies an introduction to chromatic scales on the keyboard. The exercises are presented in small, bite-sized motions at first—one hand at a time, one beat at a time—and then in a real context with the hands working together in larger and larger beat groupings.

Two chromatic scales are presented—C and F—so students can learn the basics and then duplicate the process using a slightly different "flight plan." Practicing these two sequences will build the dexterity necessary to play any chromatic scale.

You can work on the breakdown exercises with the play-along tracks either individually or combine them all for the Full Sequence.

GENERAL TECHNIQUE TIPS

- Keep mallet heights and grip consistent.
- See the scale through its anchor points.
- Pay attention to where you are striking the bars.
- Follow the stickings.

Chromatic Scales – C

BREAKDOWN ONE

One Beat (Up, then Down) This exercise breaks up the chromatic scale one beat at a time one hand at a time over one octave—first up, then down. Keep a consistent quality stroke and pay attention to the shape your hands make. Get to know the "anchor points" (i.e., start/stop points from one short phrase to the next).

Play-along Tracks

64 - SLOW – 96 bpm (00'46")
65 - MEDIUM – 104 bpm (00'43")
66 - FAST – 120 bpm (00'37")

BREAKDOWN TWO

Two-Beat (with "turnaround") This exercise breaks up the chromatic scale by creating a "turnaround." Notice again where the anchor points are. Your hands move up and down the same notes, so remember that when planning your mallets' flight path!

Play-along Tracks

67 - SLOW – 96 bpm (00'34")
68 - MEDIUM – 104 bpm (00'32")
69 - FAST – 120 bpm (00'29")

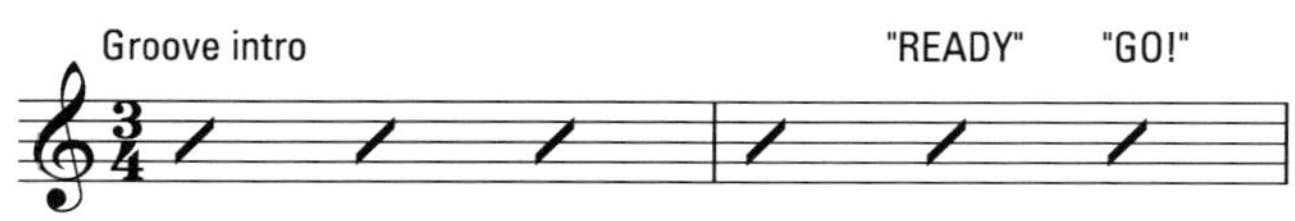

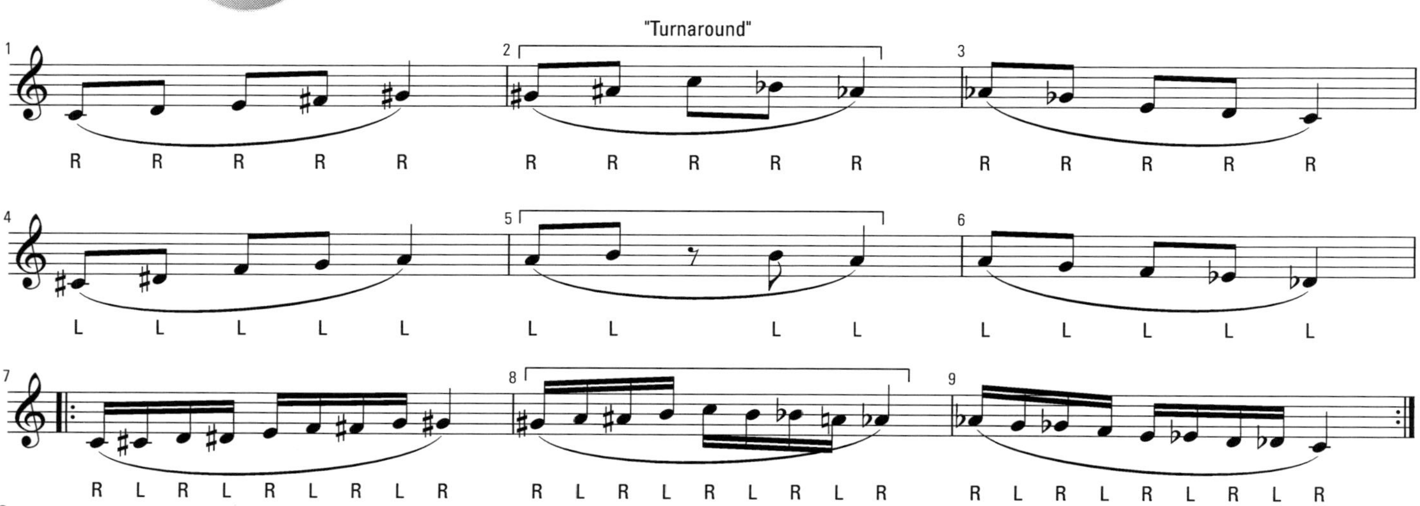

BREAKDOWN THREE

One Octave (Up, then Down) This exercise will take you all the way up the chromatic scale, stopping at the top. Recall the anchor points from the previous breakdowns!

Play-along Tracks
70 - SLOW – 96 bpm (00'32")
71 - MEDIUM – 104 bpm (00'31")
72 - FAST – 120 bpm (00'30")

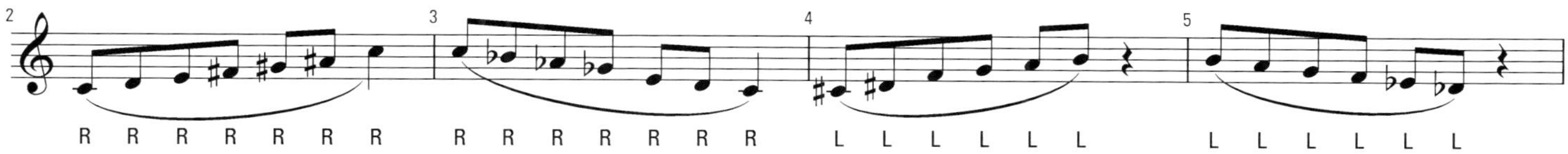

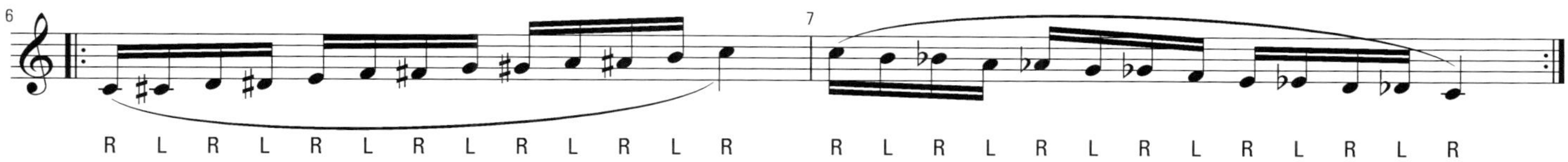

BREAKDOWN FOUR

One Octave (Non-stop) This exercise will take you all the way up and down the chromatic scale without stopping at the top.

Play-along Tracks
73 - SLOW – 96 bpm (00'45")
74 - MEDIUM – 104 bpm (00'42")
75 - FAST – 120 bpm (00'40")

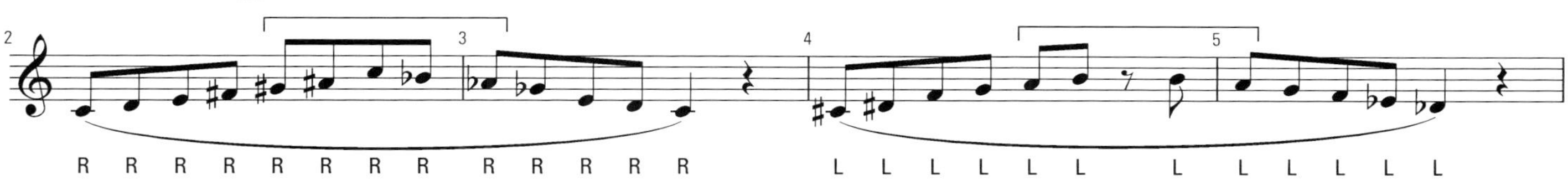

FULL SEQUENCE

For the Full Sequence, play all of the above breakdowns in one pass!

Play-along Tracks
76 - SLOW – 96 bpm (02'15")
77 - MEDIUM – 104 bpm (02'05")
78 - FAST – 120 bpm (01'49")

Chromatic Scales – F

BREAKDOWN ONE

One Beat (Up, then Down) This exercise breaks up the chromatic scale one beat at a time one hand at a time over one octave—first up, then down. Keep a consistent quality stroke and pay attention to the shape your hands make. Get to know the "anchor points" (i.e., start/stop points from one short phrase to the next).

Play-along Tracks
79 - SLOW – 96 bpm (00'46")
80 - MEDIUM – 104 bpm (00'43")
81 - FAST – 120 bpm (00'37")

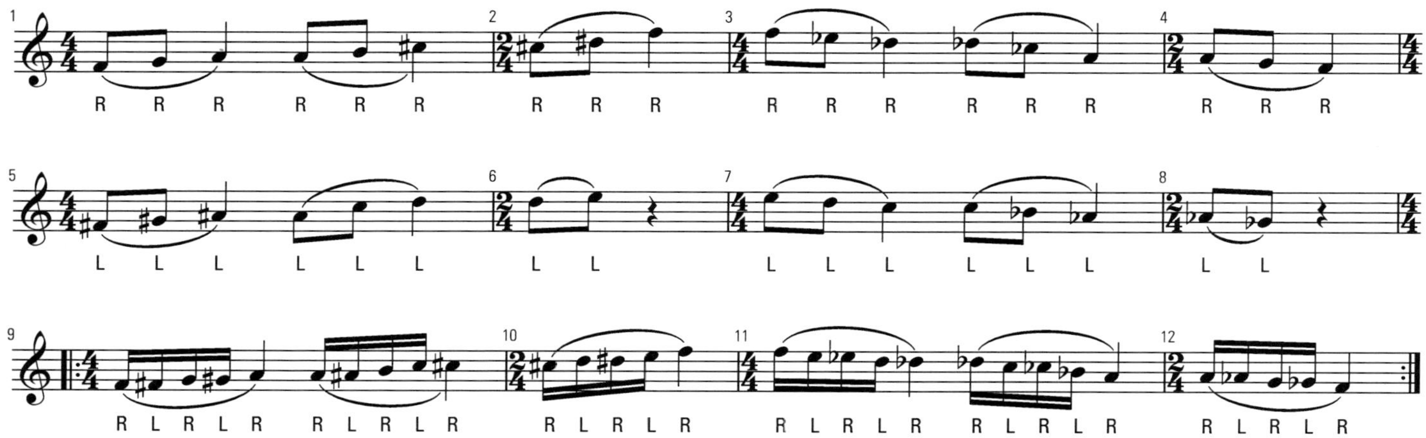

BREAKDOWN TWO

Two-Beat (with "turnaround") This exercise breaks up the chromatic scale by creating a "turnaround." Notice again where the anchor points are. Your hands move up and down the same notes, so remember that when planning your mallets' flight path!

Play-along Tracks
82 - SLOW – 96 bpm (00'34")
83 - MEDIUM – 104 bpm (00'32")
84 - FAST – 120 bpm (00'29")

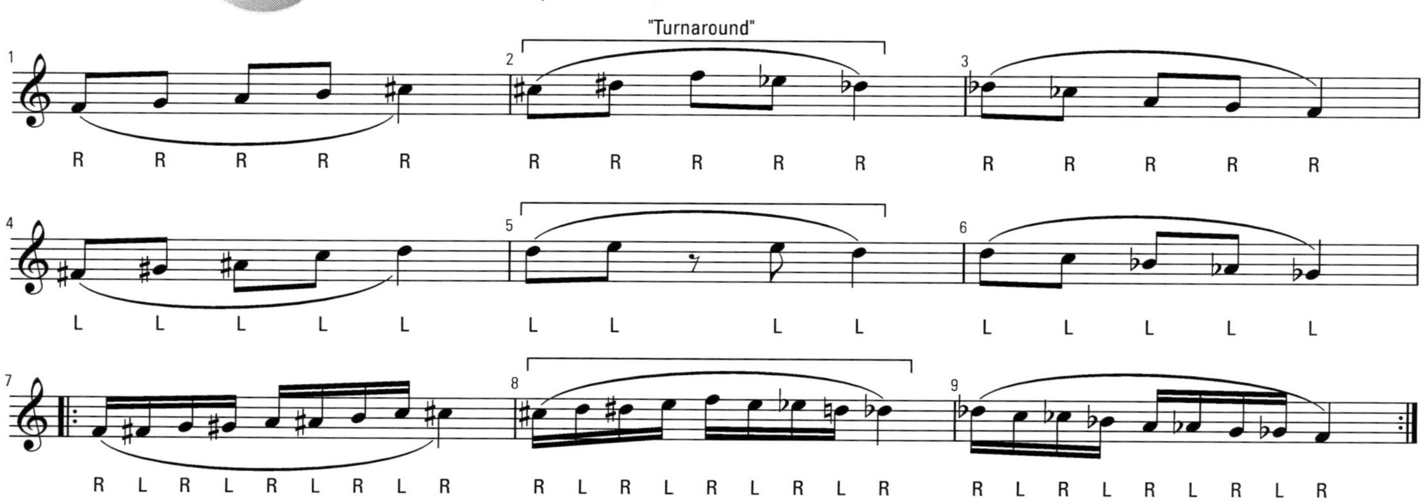

BREAKDOWN THREE

One Octave (Up, then Down) This exercise will take you all the way up the chromatic scale, stopping at the top. Recall the anchor points from the previous breakdowns!

Play-along Tracks
85 - SLOW – 96 bpm (00'32")
86 - MEDIUM – 104 bpm (00'31")
87 - FAST – 120 bpm (00'30")

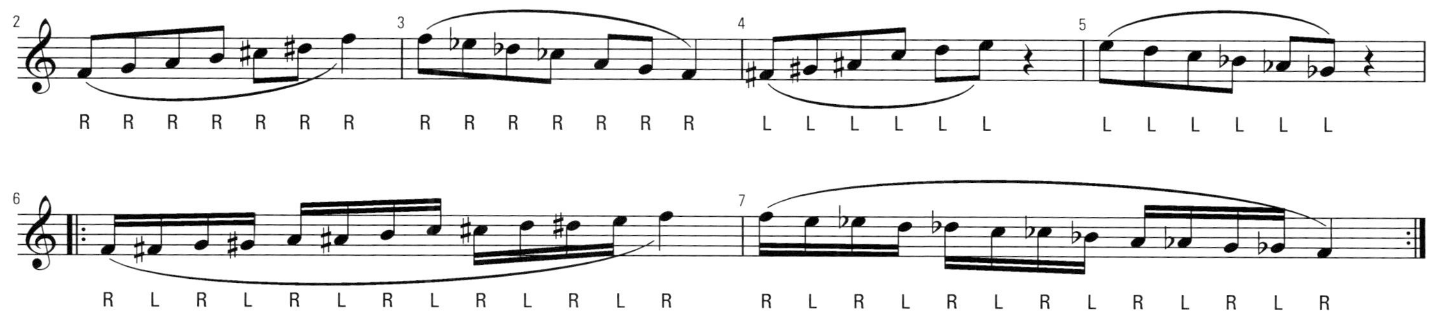

BREAKDOWN FOUR

One Octave (Non-stop) This exercise will take you all the way up and down the chromatic scale without stopping at the top.

Play-along Tracks
88 - SLOW – 96 bpm (00'45")
89 - MEDIUM – 104 bpm (00'42")
90 - FAST – 120 bpm (00'40")

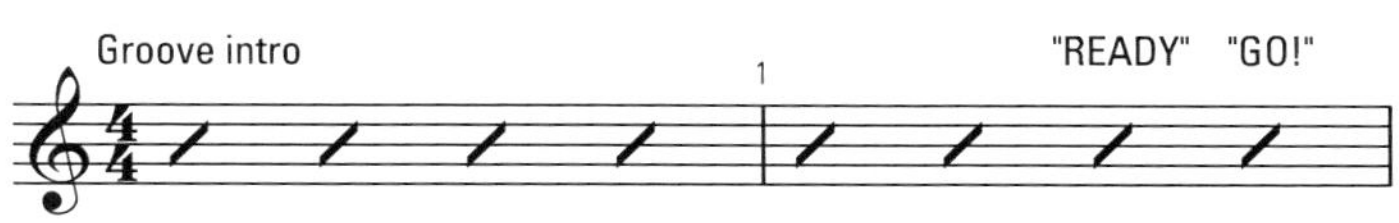

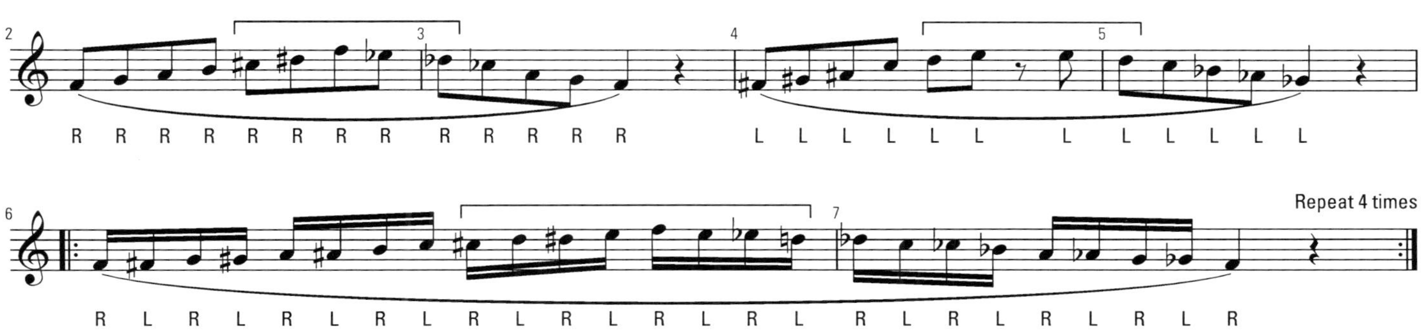

FULL SEQUENCE

For the Full Sequence, play all of the above breakdowns in one pass!

Play-along Tracks
91 - SLOW – 96 bpm (02'15")
92 - MEDIUM – 104 bpm (02'05")
93 - FAST – 120 bpm (01'49")

FIVE
MINUTE
DRILL
FIVE
MINUTE

DATA TRACKING TOOLS

We believe a solid practice routine is key to making real progress in any endeavor, musical or otherwise. Most seasoned educators, coaches, personal trainers, dieticians—you name it—acknowledge data tracking as a fundamental tool on the path to achieving mastery. For this reason, we have included a couple data tracking tools to help you make this a healthy habit of your own!

To access these tools, open the folder called "Data Tracking Tools" on your CD-ROM and locate the two printable PDF charts inside. Print as many of them as you like and as often as you need!

Remember that these tools will only be as helpful as the consistency with which you use them. Recording your progress only takes a moment, and those moments over time can help give you a clear picture of how far you've come!

TEACHERS

Progress Chart

This chart was designed to be used by the **teacher** in the classroom and will help track students' progress on a weekly basis throughout the year. Indicate the speed—**S** for Slow, **M** for Medium, **F** for Fast—of the play-along track you used for a particular exercise in the approrpriate column. We highly recommend starting all new concepts at the Slow speed while having students count out loud.

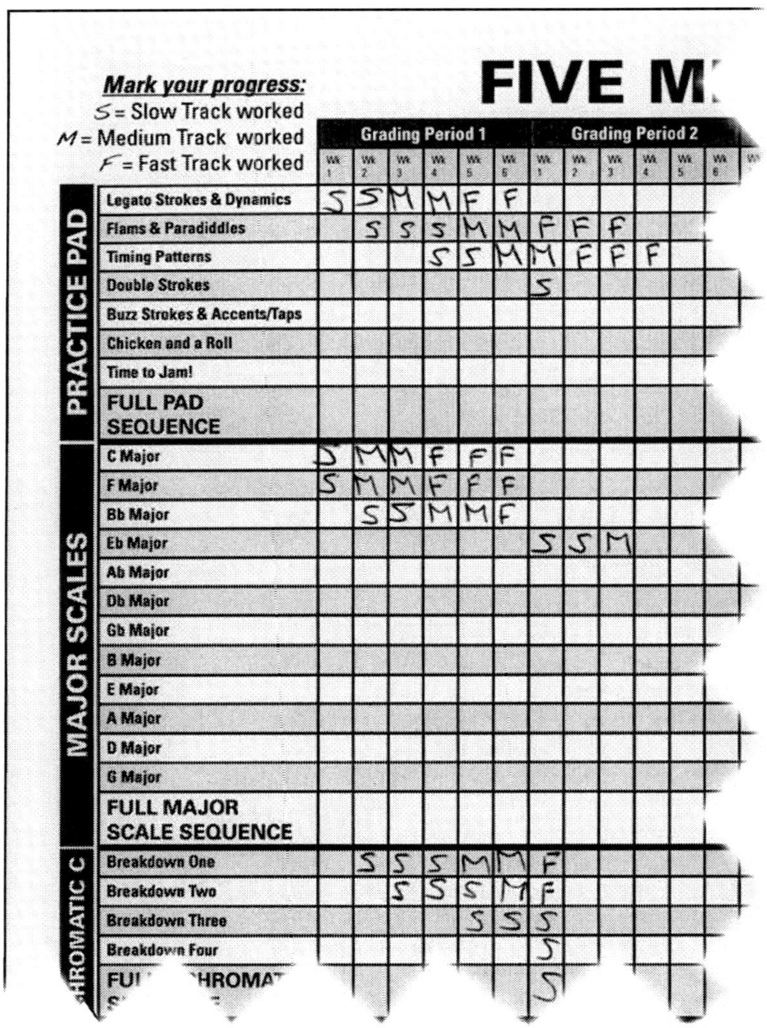

STUDENTS

Weekly Practice Log

This chart was designed to be used by **individual students** to help track their daily practice routines and habits. It is based around a 6-day practice regimen...a day off never hurt anyone! We recommend 30 minutes a day in order to see steady progress.

Remember that *some* practice is better than *no* practice. If you don't have time to practice for a full 30 minutes, do what you can and log the results anyway. Every little bit helps!

FIVE MINUTE DRILL *Weekly Practice Log*

Mark your progress:
S = Slow Track worked
M = Medium Track worked
F = Fast Track worked

Student Name: Johnny "Stix" McJamband

	Practice Pad	Major Scales	Chromatic Scales	Results
Day 1 1/7/13 Date	[M] Legato Strokes & Dynamics [M] Flams & Paradiddles [S] Timing Patterns [ ] Double Strokes [ ] Buzz Strokes & Accents [ ] Chicken and a Roll [ ] Time to Jam! [ ] **Full Pad Sequence**	[F] C [ ] Gb [M] F [ ] B [S] Bb [ ] E [ ] Eb [ ] A [ ] Ab [ ] D [ ] Db [ ] G [ ] **Full Major Sequence**	Circle one: (**C to C**) **F to F** [S] Breakdown One [S] Breakdown Two [S] Breakdown Three [S] Breakdown Four [S] **Full Chromatic Sequence**	*Notes:* I rock *Did you accomplish your goal?* [X] Yes [ ] No
	Minutes Worked: 10	Minutes Worked: 10	Minutes Worked: 10	**Total Minutes:**
Day 2 1/8/13 Date	[F] Legato Strokes & Dynamics [M] Flams & Paradiddles [M] Timing Patterns [S] Double Strokes [ ] Buzz Strokes & Accents [ ] Chicken and a Roll [ ] Time to Jam! [ ] **Full Pad Sequence**	[ ] C [ ] Gb [ ] F [ ] B [ ] Bb [ ] E [ ] Eb [ ] A [ ] Ab [ ] D [ ] Db [ ] G [ ] **Full Major Sequence**	Circle one: (**C to C**) **F to F** [M] Breakdown One [M] Breakdown Two [M] Breakdown Three [M] Breakdown Four [S] **Full Chromatic Sequence**	*Notes:* I didn't get to major scales today ☹ *Did you accomplish your goal?* [ ] Yes [X] No
	Minutes Worked: 15	Minutes Worked: 0	Minutes Worked: 15	**Total Minutes:** 30
Day 3 1/10/13 Date	[F] Legato Strokes & Dynamics [F] Flams & Paradiddles [F] Timing Patterns [F] Double Strokes [S] Buzz Strokes & Accents [ ] Chicken and a Roll [ ] Time to Jam! [ ] **Full Pad Sequence**	[F] C [ ] Gb [F] F [ ] B [M] Bb [ ] E [M] Eb [ ] A [S] Ab [ ] D [ ] Db [ ] G [ ] **Full Major Sequence**	Circle one: **C to C** (**F to F**) [S] Breakdown One [S] Breakdown Two [S] Breakdown Three [ ] Breakdown Four [ ] **Full Chromatic Sequence**	*Notes:* I'm scared of Db! *Did you accomplish your goal?* [X] Yes [ ] No
	Minutes Worked: 10	Minutes Worked: 15	Minutes Worked:	**Total Minutes:** 30